3/01

The Red–Green
coalition in

D0714237

MANCHESTER
UNIVERSITY PRESS

ISSUES IN GERMAN POLITICS
Edited by
Professor Charlie Jeffery, Institute for German Studies
Dr Charlie Lees, University of Sussex

Issues in German Politics is a major new series on contemporary Germany. Focusing on the post-unity era, it presents concise, scholarly analyses of the forces driving change in domestic politics and foreign policy. Key themes will be the continuing legacies of German unification and controversies surrounding Germany's role and power in Europe. The series includes contributions from political science, international relations and political economy.

Already published:

Bulmer, Jeffery and Paterson: *Germany's European diplomacy: Shaping the regional milieu*

Harding and Paterson: *The future of the German economy: An end to the miracle?*

Hyde-Price: *Germany and European order: Enlarging NATO and the EU*

The Red–Green coalition in Germany

Politics, personalities and power

Charles Lees

Manchester University Press

Manchester and New York

Distributed exclusively in the USA by Palgrave

Published by Manchester University Press
Oxford Road, Manchester M13 9NR, UK
and Room 400, 175 Fifth Avenue, New York, NY 10010, USA
http/www.manchesteruniversitypress.co.uk

Distributed exclusively in the USA by
Palgrave, 175 Fifth Avenue, New York,
NY 10010,USA

Distributed exclusively in Canada by
UBC Press, University of British Columbia, 2029 West Mall,
Vancouver, BC, Canada V6T 1Z2

British Library Cataloguing-in-Publication Data
A catalogue record for this book is available from the British Library

Library of Congress Cataloging-in-Publication Data applied for

ISBN 0 7190 5838 4 *hardback*
0 7190 5839 2 *paperback*

First published 2000

09 08 07 06 05 04 03 02 01 00   10 9 8 7 6 5 4 3 2 1

Typeset in Minion
by Northern Phototypesetting Co. Ltd, Bolton
Printed in Great Britain
by Bell & Bain Ltd, Glasgow

FOR KIRSTEN

Contents

Acknowledgements

The ideas that underpin this thesis are the culmination of over 10 years of active interest in the SPD and Greens in the Federal Republic of Germany, first as a resident of Berlin in the late 1980s and more recently as an academic.

I wish to thank my colleagues, friends and family for their support and encouragement. Paul Taggart, Ted Tapper and colleagues at the University of Sussex; Willie Paterson, Charlie Jeffery and David Marsh at the University of Birmingham; Albert Weale at the University of Essex; Stephen Padgett at the University of Strathclyde; Simon Green at the University of Portsmouth; Michael Kreile and colleagues at the Humboldt University in Berlin; Bernard Blanke and colleagues at the University of Hannover; the officials in the Berlin and Lower Saxony Environment Ministries, as well as the numerous local SPD and Green party members and others who so generously gave up their time to speak to me, often at short notice; the German Academic Exchange Service (DAAD) for providing generous financial support for my fieldwork in Germany; and everyone at the Manchester University Press. I would also like to thank Bernard and Gesa, Maurice and Simone, Piers and Alain, and Chris for friendship and help along the way. Special thanks as well to Leo and June Lees for reading early drafts of this book.

My biggest debt of gratitude goes to my wife, Kirsten Barnes, for her love and support throughout, and for proof-reading beyond the call of duty! It is to her that this book is dedicated.

Charles Lees,
Brighton, August 2000

1
Introduction

On 27 September 1998, the Social Democratic Party (SPD) won the Bundestag elections. After sixteen years of opposition, the party had clawed its way back to the brink of power. Now they had to find a suitable coalition partner – and they made it clear that this could be the Greens.

The Greens had come in from the cold. It had been fourteen years earlier, in 1983, when the delegates of this self-proclaimed 'anti-party party' had first taken their seats in the Bundestag. With its roots in the student protests of the late 1960s, the neo-communist 'K-groups' of the early 1970s, and the popular environmental and peace movements of the late 1970s and early 1980s, the Greens gate-crashed the Federal Republic's cosy political consensus and offered a new kind of politics. In the intervening years ideological moderation inevitably set in and, at the level of the German states, the Greens became an established party of government. At the Federal level the Greens remained an outsider party and the idea of their participating in national government alarmed the political establishment. It also alarmed many of their own supporters, who preferred the purity of perpetual opposition to the compromise and horse-trading of government.

Now the Greens had a choice to make: to remain an anti-party party and stay true to the ideals of the movements from which they had come, or to grasp the opportunity that now presented itself. The chance might never come again and the Greens' leading lights, veterans of the so-called '68er' generation, were not getting any younger. To pass up this chance of real power – in the knowledge that it might not come again – would be a bitter pill indeed. For them the choice was clear.

Aims, structure and methods

This book explains how the Greens got to the position where they could make such a choice and why they came to the choice they made. In making that choice the Greens helped usher in a new political era – not just for Germany but for Europe as a whole. The defeat of Helmut Kohl meant that one of the great post-war statesmen left the world stage, to be replaced with what appeared to many observers to be an untested political force with no previous experience of national government. Much has been written about the political antecedents of the Greens, and these volatile origins have been vividly contrasted with the SPD's relatively staid political culture and record in government. As a result, opinion formers on both sides of the Atlantic speculated that a Red–Green coalition in Berlin could be inherently unstable, with profound political and economic implications for Germany and Europe. In the event Joschka Fischer's appointment to the post of first Green Foreign Minister in the history of the Federal Republic caused very little concern at home or abroad. This was owing to his reputation as a moderate and the countervailing weight of the SPD – particularly the Chancellor's Office – within the coalition. The almost seamless replacement of the outgoing Conservative-Liberal administration with the new Red–Green coalition was hailed as further evidence of the growing maturity and stability of the Federal Republic.

The first year of Red–Green government was a stormy one. The 'surprise' resignation of SPD Finance Minister Oskar Lafontaine appeared, at the time at least, to be a significant blow. Moreover, the low-key intergovernmental row prompted by Green Environment Minister Jürgen Trittin's attempt to unilaterally cancel contracts for the re-processing of spent German fuel rods in France and the United Kingdom was seen as evidence of the coalition's lack of experience. In addition, the crisis in Kosovo put enormous strain on the coalition. Fault lines opened up not only between the parties – with the Greens broadly speaking less inclined to support North Atlantic Treaty Organisation (NATO) policy than the SPD – but within and across them.

Despite a bumpy first year, Schröder and his team remained in office. Yet many questions remain to be answered. Does Schröder know where his coalition is going? Does he have a clear set of political objectives and can he rely on his Green coalition partners to achieve them? When we consider these questions, what can we learn from the record of Red–Green political co-operation in the German states? The key to these questions lies in the stability of the relationship between the SPD and the Greens and, in particular, the extent to which Greens have assumed a 'normal' political role within the party system. Such a normal role would mean that their behaviour can be predicted in much the same way as one can predict the behaviour of, say, a typical Western European Social Democratic, Christian Democratic or Liberal party. All parties have their own preferences, be they instrumental (office-seeking) and/or ideological (related to policy processes and outcomes), but in mature democracies, what one could call mainstream parties, increasingly share two common characteristics.

The first is that of ideological convergence, which has come about partly as result of wider systemic changes. For the left/centre-left, the end of the cold war and the collapse of the former Soviet Union has taken much of the heat out of the ideological rivalry that has hobbled it since the 'critical juncture' of the Russian Revolution and the creation of the Third International (Lipset and Rokkan, 1967). Crucial to this has been the abject failure of the Soviet model of political and economic organisation – based on democratic centralism and the command economy – and the subsequent loss of credibility of a distinctive communist platform. These events have also served to narrow the gap between the left/centre-left and the centre-right.

The second characteristic is that of elite dominance, with parties increasingly conforming to what Katz and Mair (1995) refer to as a 'cartel party' model of party organisation. Across Europe, party structures have become increasingly centralised. Office-holding politicians have become increasingly alienated from their extra-parliamentary membership which, whilst retaining a high symbolic value as the legitimator of elites, is increasingly by-passed by them. This is particularly the case when elites pursue co-operative strategies with elites from other parties, or from 'non-traditional' client groups, such as – in the case of Social Democratic parties – big business. The combined effect of these two trends is that party elites are less restrained by ideology, be it within the party system or within the hearts of their grass roots' members. As a result of the down-playing of ideological differences and the marginalisation of the ordinary membership, it has become easier for elites to pursue strategies of political co-operation.

In this book I argue that these processes have clearly taken place within and between the SPD and the Greens. They have shaped the SPD's response to electoral realignment and to new political competitors (such as the Greens and, indeed, the Party of Democratic Socialism (PDS)), and were crucial in determining the outcome of the 'realo-fundi' conflict within the Green party. In both instances, party elites displayed a willingness to push for a co-operative strategy in the face of grass-roots resistance to the Red–Green 'project'. Why this has been the case is a subject for debate and one's own particular judgement. For instance, scholars who suspect that all parties eventually succumb to what Michels (1970) called 'the iron law of oligarchy' may wish to focus primarily on internal party organisation through the theoretical lens of elite theory. In many ways any such choice is arbitrary. As Weale observes, one's choice of model – or 'idiom of analysis' as he calls them – is down to the individual analyst in as much as he or she judges it to 'provide a way of talking about, and therefore understanding, political processes'. Weale goes on to stress that not only are such idioms not mutually exclusive but their internal components are often only loosely related to each other. As a result, Weale suggests that the analyst may have to draw upon a quite heterogeneous literature, given that 'there sometimes is no canonical source to which one can go' (1992: 38).

This book focuses on coalition theory as a means of explaining Red–Green coalitions in Germany, a choice of idiom which is as arbitrary as any. It is based upon the assumption that within the generic term 'coalition theory', there is a model, or set of models, that provides both a predictive and explanatory account of coalition behaviour. I have chosen to build on four established models from the literature. These are Riker's (1962) 'minimum/minimal-winning' model, Axelrod's (1970) 'minimal connected winning' model, de Swaan's (1973) concept of the 'median legislator' and the Shepsle's (1979) notion of 'structure induced equilibrium'. The notions behind these idioms are explained in more detail in Chapter 2, in which they are used heuristically to demonstrate an ideal type, or 'Red–Green model', of coalition building, which I argue has developed over time at the level of the individual German state since the early 1980s.

An historical overview of Red–Green co-operation at state level from the early 1980s until the present day is given in Chapter 3. Included in this account is the period of unofficial co-operation between the SPD and Greens in Hamburg and Hessen in the early 1980s, as well as formal Red–Green coalitions in Hessen, West Berlin, Niedersachsen, Mecklenburg-Vorpommern and Nordrhein-Westfalen, and the minority coalition ('tolerated' by the PDS) in Saxony-Anhalt. In addition it looks briefly at the so-called 'Traffic-Light' coalitions in Brandenburg (with Alliance 90 and the FDP) and Bremen (with the Greens and the Free Democratic Party (FDP)).

Chapters 4 and 5 develop in more detail the themes raised in Chapter 3 and examine the idea of a 'Red–Green model' by focusing on two case studies from the German states. An explanation of why the book uses case studies is given in Chapter 2, but the case study format provides a useful means of bringing alive what would otherwise be no more than an abstract model. In so doing it also tells two interesting political 'stories', in which many of the players are now on the national stage and will be familiar to readers. The cases were chosen with three criteria in mind. First, they are geographically well dispersed within the Federal Republic and not limited to one particular region and/or political culture. Second, they span the period before and after German unification and thus encompass the changes that have taken place within the party system as a whole during the last ten years. Third, they were in place long enough for their record to be objectively assessed. The cases are West Berlin (1989–90) and Niedersachsen (1990–94).

The Red–Green coalition of 1989–90 in West Berlin was relatively short lived but was in place during the period running up to and including the unification of Germany. Thus, a coalition that formed in what was in many ways a political backwater – and where some degree of political risk taking was possible – ended in the full glare of the national (and even international) spotlight as the city took centre stage in world events. Moreover, a coalition that was elected to govern a relatively prosperous 'West German' city of just over two million inhabitants soon became responsible for a socially and economically divided metropolis of almost double that number. It will be shown that the themes which had previously bound the coalition together (such as the environment, nuclear and conventional disarmament and other 'quality-of-life' issues) were superseded by more urgent concerns (such as unification, nationalism and the collapse of the economy in Eastern Germany). The differing responses of the Berlin 'Alternative Liste' (as the local Greens were then called) and the SPD to these concerns was to ultimately undermine the coalition and vividly demonstrates the effect of intra- and inter-party divisions over ideology and strategy, the potential for personality clashes and the destructive power of what Harold Macmillan famously referred to as 'events'. In addition, the case is interesting because it has been the subject of relatively little research.

In contrast, the 1990–94 Red–Green coalition in Niedersachsen was widely regarded as successful and would probably have been renewed, if the electoral arithmetic had made it neccessary, following the elections in March of 1994. The case provides a useful insight into the political skills and personal style of Gerhard Schröder in his previous post as Minister President of Niedersachsen and of the then leader of the Niedersachsen Greens Jürgen Trittin. Together with the impressive Joschka Fischer the three men have emerged as the most visible figures within the national coalition, and the case study provides pointers to the shape and tone of its internal politics. Like Berlin, the Niedersachsen coalition has been the subject of little research.

The second half of the book takes a closer look at Chancellor Gerhard Schröder's Red–Green coalition. Chapter 6 examines the period running up to the 1998 Bundestag elections, with an emphasis on the efforts made by the two parties to narrow the ideological distance between them and, at the same time, mobilise their own core electorate. Included in the chapter is an account of the internal political battle between Schröder and Oskar Lafontaine to secure the SPD's nomination as Chancellor-candidate, and the more low-profile struggle between Joschka Fischer and Jürgen Trittin to set the ideological compass of the Greens in the run up to the elections. The chapter also includes a brief description of the two parties campaign strategies. Chapter 7 examines the two parties' programmes, coalition strategies and the period of coalition bargaining following the elections. In particular, it assesses the division of Ministerial portfolios between the two parties in the light of the experience of deals at the sub-national level. Following on from this, Chapter 8 gives an account of the coalition's first year in power. Areas emphasised include economic and fiscal policy, nuclear policy, citizenship reform, the Kosovan crisis and the so-called 'New Centre' (Germany's equivalent of the Third Way). The chapter highlights the roles of Schröder, Lafontaine, Fischer and Trittin in setting the tone of the coalition's first year.

The book concludes by assessing the coalition's record to date, as well as the suitability of the 'Red–Green model' as a template for political cooperation at the national level. It raises questions about the future direction of the coalition and asks if we are any nearer to knowing the direction Chancellor Schröder wants to take it.

2
Explaining Red–Green coalitions

Idioms of analysis

A large and heterogeneous literature exists relating to coalition behaviour. The field is conceptually diverse and many of the more important models within the genre are to some extent contradictory. Moreover, theorists have often taken different aspects of coalition behaviour as their starting point. For instance, the bulk of the early literature was primarily concerned with the process of coalition formation and paid little attention to the degree to which such coalitions were successfully maintained. The reason for this was that much of the early modelling relied upon a strictly game-theoretical approach and the majority of such models took an 'office-seeking' perspective, which either ignored or down-graded the policy dimension as a formation criteria. But once we examine why some coalitions are more durable than others over time, the idea that office-seeking motives are the only decisive criteria within the bargaining process becomes very hard to sustain. For instance, if we assume that office seeking is the only reason such coalitions form, it would be reasonable to ask why they break down at all, given that some degree of equilibrium has been established within which all agents in the coalition have achieved office. Why would such a coalition not go on in perpetuity rather than breaking down and allowing a rival coalition of agents to gain office? One reply to this would be to point out that parties within the coalition are acting rationally and may actually be maximising their office seeking chances over the long run. For instance, they might expect to be a member of any rival coalition that forms or, alternatively, they may calculate that the rival coalition will not last long and that they have a good chance of soon returning to office in an enhanced position. In both cases, it could be argued that office seeking is still the dominant criterion for explaining the behaviour of these parties. Such questions highlight the interplay between office seeking and ideology when looking at coalition behaviour. Although ideology has declined in importance over recent years, historically it has had a relatively important role in European party systems, at least compared with the limited role of ideological conflict in the United States (where the bulk of theoretical work has been carried out). Thus, in order to explain coalition behaviour within the context-rich environment found in European party systems, it is essential to include a 'policy dimension' and, in the case of Red–Green coalitions, environmental policy can be assumed to play an important role. It is the policy area most closely identified with the Greens and is at the core of their own self-identity and of external perceptions of them.

As already noted, Weale suggests that even when working within one idiom of analysis, the analyst may have to draw upon a quite heterogeneous literature, and his caveats are particularly germane to the broad sweep of literature related to coalition theory. As Laver and Schofield observe, there have traditionally been two distinct and divergent 'traditions' within coalition theory which 'are by now so far apart that they have almost nothing to contribute to one another' (1990: 10–11). These traditions can be broadly classified as the game-theoretical (or formal-deductive) and 'European politics' (primarily inductive) schools. In recent years, scholars such as Laver and Schofield (1990) and Budge and Keman (1990) have attempted to bridge this gulf and incorporate empirical and contextual variables into their theoretical modelling. All such attempts involve an implicit trade-off between the rigidity of formal deductive modelling and the social scientist's desire to achieve a good empirical 'fit' which brings us further in our understanding.

Although not a coalition theory in itself, the early models of coalition formation owed a lot to the work of Anthony Downs. In his *An Economic Theory of Democracy* (1957), Downs built upon the game-theoretical work of von Neumann and Morgenstern (1947) and Savage (1954) and constructed a formal theory of politics. Central to Down's theory was the prior assumption that office seeking is the ultimate goal of political strategy, in that 'parties formulate policies in order to win elections, rather than win elections in order to formulate policies' (Downs, 1957: 28). Thus, although Downs acknowledged the existence of a policy dimension to political competition, he saw it as secondary to the parties' main preoccupation with maximising votes in order to win elections and acquire office. In order to do this, office-seeking parties compete for the 'median voter', which in most party systems is to be found at the political centre of a given polity.

The debt that early coalition theorists owed to Downs' theory is acknowledged by William Riker in his *The Theory of Political Coalitions*, in which he states that Downs' book is 'one of the half-dozen outstanding works of political theory in this century' (1962: 33). Riker builds upon Downs' work to construct a predictive model of coalition formation in which office seeking plays a central role. The focus of Riker's model lies with the strategies adopted by the parties, who are assumed to be rational actors, as they attempt to gain admission to any coalition that may form. This process takes place within a game-theoretical environment that is both 'constant sum' (limited in size and scope) and 'zero-sum' (one player's gain diminishes the potential utility of all other players). Each player is assigned a 'weight' within the bargaining process, determined by the resources that the players bring to any potential coalition. Given that office seeking rather than policy is assumed to be the central formation criterion, these resources take the form of votes, parliamentary seats or power. Riker predicts that players will try to create coalitions that are only as large as they believe will ensure winning. In its pure theoretical form, such a 'minimal winning' coalition would be so small as to maximise the payoffs (which are assumed to be a function of each player's weight) to each coalition member. With repeated 'plays' of the bargaining game there would be a tendency towards the smallest subset of potential minimal winning coalitions, towards a 'minimum winning' coalition of 50 per cent plus one vote. Like Downs, Riker assumes that parties are motivated by the desire to acquire office rather than to formulate or implement policy. This assumption is further refined in the related work of William Gamson, who argues that parties are intent on 'maximising the ratio of (their) resources to the total resources of the coalition' and that 'the lower the total resources, the greater will be (their) share. Thus … [they] will favour the 'cheapest winning' coalition' (1961: 376). This means that parties would prefer to be a big fish in a small pond rather than be a 'junior' partner in a bigger coalition, even when the benefits of doing so are broadly comparable.

The formal nature of Riker and Gamson's two models have attracted much criticism on epistemological grounds. The most commonly cited criticism is that the focus upon office seeking makes these models effectively 'policy blind' (Laver and Schofield, 1990: 90) and therefore unrealistic. One possible riposte to this accusation would be along the lines of Milton Friedman's (1953) 'billiard ball' argument that it is not the realism of a model's assumptions that are important when judging the adequacy of a theory but rather the fit between its logical consequences and the actual phenomena under study. A similar argument is made by Riker and Ordeshook, who defend positivism in political science in general by asserting that it is 'just as important to generate and test out new theories as to investigate obvious phenomena' (1973: xi). Nevertheless, Riker and Gamson's models have a modest record in predicting real outcomes of coalition bargaining. For instance, Eric Browne tested all three models against data drawn from thirteen parliamentary democracies covering the period 1945–70 and found that they correctly predicted only 8 per cent of the actual outcomes of coalition bargaining during this period. Nevertheless, Browne does point out that other tests have supported their underlying assumptions (1973: 17–31), even if their predictive power leaves something to be desired.

Laver and Schofield also defend the predictive power of the minimal winning hypothesis, especially Riker's model. With reference to data drawn from European democracies between 1945 and 1987, they point out that, although only 35 per cent of actual coalition outcomes were cor-rectly predicted, the number of potential coalition formations that might have arisen in such multi-party legislatures is exponentially higher. Given the huge number of possible outcomes, to correctly predict the actual outcome once in every three trials is a quite respectable achievement (1990: 70–93).

These observations are a reminder that, when testing the predictive power of the three theories against empirical data that have already been gathered, one must remember that in reality these are not predictions at all but rather what Lawrence Dodd has called 'postdictions' (1976: 21). In any given specific case, one possesses knowledge of both previous bar-gaining outcomes and the actual outcomes under study. In such circum-stances, and by process of inductive reasoning, a given outcome may appear fairly self-evident. However, if one reasons deductively – and therefore discounts the institutionally specific information we all possess – any process of coalition formation in a multi-party environment is sim-ply an n-person game (involving more than two players) which generates exponential outcomes as players are added. Martin Schubik's general for-mulation for such games vividly demonstrates how unwieldy they can become as additional players are added. Even when either player only makes a 'yes/no' decision about whether to join a coalition, a two-person game of this nature will generate three possible outcomes (yes/yes, no/no, yes/no). If we use the analogy of a multi-party system, the addition of an extra player generates seven outcomes, a fourth fifteen, a fifth thirty one and so on to the point that ten players generated a potential 1,023 outcomes (Schubik, 1967: 249, cited in Hinckley, 1981: 24).

The fact that such pure office-seeking accounts of coalition formation have enjoyed only partial success as predictors of actual outcomes has led scholars such as Bogdanor (1983), von Beyme (1984) and Pridham (1986) to conclude that the use of such models is misguided, at least when looking at European party systems. The gist of their arguments is that not only are pure office-seeking accounts conceptually flawed in their neglect of the policy dimension, but also that these explanatory shortcomings are not compensated for by the models' predictive power. Pure office-seeking models of coalition formation retain their adherents, but the assumptions that underpin them are essentially contested. It is therefore no surprise that even theorists who remain convinced of the need for formal modelling went on to bring in a policy dimension.

Robert Axelrod's *Conflict of Interest* (1970) is one of the most frequently cited early examples of this approach. Axelrod assumes that, whilst office seeking remains the central strategic goal of all players, the members of the successful coalition will ideally be adjacent to one another along a single Downsian left–right ideological dimension. Such 'minimal connected winning' coalitions are assumed to be as large as necessary to secure a majority in the legislature, and as adjacent as possible to minimise the potential for conflicts of interest within the coalition. There are three main objections to the assumptions inherent in Axelrod's model. First, although minimal connected winning predictions did better than minimal winning predictions with regard to actual outcomes of Cabinet formation in post-war Europe, their success rate was only 20 per cent. This compares badly with the 12 per cent success rate which is achieved by chance (Laver and Schofield, 1990: 98). Second, the underlying assumption that minimal connected winning coalitions have lower levels of conflicts of interest has been empirically challenged by Browne, Gleiber and Mashoba (1984) (although they do not question the model's predictive power). Finally, although Axelrod's model assumes ideological adjacency, it has no conception of the ideological distance between parties. For instance, take a right-leaning legislature in which party Y is a conservative party, party X is a bourgeois/centrist party, yet parties U and T are respectively eco-socialist and Maoist, and imagine that the minimal connected winning coalition is X,U,T. Given what we know about party ideology, it is hard to credit a scenario in which even the most office-seeking bourgeois/centrist party would go into coalition with parties U and T. Moreover, Axelrod's central assumption that such a coalition would minimise conflicts of interest is hard to credit under such circumstances. In short, an effective model needs to be able to conceptualise and take into account spatial information about ideological distance between parties and across the legislature as a whole.

In his *Coalition Theories and Cabinet Formation* (1973), Abram de Swaan elaborated upon Axelrod's work in order to construct what he called the 'closed minimum range' of Cabinet formation. De Swaan's theory predicts that the winning set will comprise the minimal connected winning coalition with the smallest ideological range. The policy dimension remains a single Downsian left–right axis, running from progressivism to conservatism and all parties are assumed to have preference orderings of all potential coalitions, based upon their relative proximities to the median or 'Mparty' (of both a given coalition and within the legislature as a whole). De Swaan's theory is often referred to as the 'median legislator' or 'median party' model because it is based on the assumption that the party that controls the median legislator in any potential coalition is decisive because it blocks the axis along which any connected winning coalition must form. If a party is what de Swaan calls the 'Mparty' (median within the legislature) and 'Mparty(k)' (controlling the median legislator within a potential coalition) in all cases, then in theory any such party must be included in the winning set.

Not only do the assumptions that underpin de Swaan's model seem reasonable, but its predictive power is also better than pure office-seeking accounts of coalition formation. For instance, whereas the Riker and Gamson models correctly predicted 8 per cent of actual outcomes, de Swaan's own tests yielded a 69 per cent prediction rate of actual outcomes from data on European coalition processes (cited Browne, 1973: 76). This would appear to represent significant progress towards a formal deductive model of coalition formation that is both explanatory and possesses considerable predictive power. But as long as the size principle is retained one is confronted with the trade-off between coalition size and ideological range. De Swaan allows us to conceptualise ideological distance (albeit in a one-dimensional form), but makes no assumption as to the institutional/ideological norms that skew the process of coalition formation and act as a variable upon coalition maintenance. Thus, although they offer plausible explanations for the coalition bargaining process, office-seeking models of coalition formation fail to address the question of how coalitions are maintained and why they break down. A policy-driven theory of coalition behaviour is needed in order to explain the processes of coalition maintenance as well as coalition formation. Moreover, policy-driven accounts can be both rigorously deductive in nature or allow for a more inductive or historical-institutional approach.

Formal deductive policy-driven models of coalition behaviour are generally spatial in their conceptualisation. Most spatial theories have moved beyond the single Downsian left–right dimension and posit the idea of a multi-dimensional policy space. Just as Schubik's formula demonstrates the exponential growth of outcomes in a simple n-person game when players are added, so the imposition of one or even two additional dimensions exponentially increases the potential outcomes in a given game. Given the potential for disequilibrium, formal policy-driven models of coalition behaviour have focused upon conceptualising the processes that impose order upon voting games. More often than not, this has involved some variation upon the game-theoretical concept of the 'core' or 'barycenter' (Hanson, 1972, Hanson and Rice, 1972). In *Coalition Theories: A Logical and Empirical Critique*, Eric Browne (1973) suggests that core theory could be used to augment de Swaan's 'median legislator' model of coalition formation. Browne considers the process of calculating the mean of points in multi-dimensional space to be analogous to de Swaan's measurement of the distance of potential coalition partners from the median of that potential coalition. A weight is assigned to each party according to their position within a given policy space (as well as the number of seats they hold in the legislature) and the 'barycenter' (as Browne calls it) is calculated as the mean of these positions. The predicted coalition will be that which is winning and minimises the policy distance of members from the core.

Core theory is generally highly mathematical in nature and has been more popular with political theorists than empiricists. Keith Krehbiel's (1988) review of the field in *Legislative Studies Quarterly* provides a good introduction to its application to practical politics. In essence, core theory assumes that a point exists in n-dimensional space that minimises the preference disagreement of a specific set of players and thus dominates all other possible outcomes. The perceived benefit of being in a given coalition is based upon its members' calculation of the potential damage all players outside the coalition could do to it. Such an allocation is called the coalition's 'security level'. As the core consists of that set of preferences that are not dominated by any other, it is assumed also to be Pareto optimal (in other words, there is no other way of making a particular coalition member better off than they are without making another worse off). A core coalition may even imply a grand coalition of all the players involved and the location of the core is plotted by calculating the mean of a collection of points (representing the policy positions of the parties) within political space. The core is bound to exist in one-dimensional space, and finds an analogue in the Downs' 'median voter' or de Swaan's 'median legislator'. But as Krehbiel points out, 'simply expanding the choice space from one to two has profoundly disequilibriating consequences' (1988: 259–319) because there will always be an alternative coalition package that can block any potential winning coalition (Bacharach, 1976: 128).

This idea of an unstable core is important because it formally models a dynamic which empirical research into Red–Green coalitions has implicitly recognised: that co-operation between the SPD and Greens has been the result of the 'selective emphasis' of the post-materialist dimension of ideology. This is no surprise, given the Greens' origins within the new social movements, and reflects the dominant strand of their ideology. However, in the case of the SPD, this is only part of their ideological make up and they retain the ability to compete and co-operate with other parties along the materialist ideological dimension – in other words, concerning the so-called 'bread and butter issues' such as economic growth, redistribution of wealth, etc. Thus, core theory has proved attractive to political scientists because it has the potential to allow for the varying degrees of stability that are characteristic of democracy. But it is dogged by the potential for permanent disequilibrium when the policy space is expanded beyond the single Downsian left–right dimension. Although the phenomenon of constantly shifting coalitions and allegiances is not unknown in practical politics (consider post-war Italy for instance), it is at odds with the experience of most Western democracies, which are characterised by coalitions which manage to maintain themselves over time. In other words, how does one explain the persistence of such stable institutions?

In an article in the *American Journal of Political Science*, Kenneth Shepsle (1979) attempts to factor in the institutional context whilst retaining a formal deductive approach to the problem. Shepsle concentrates upon the role of committees (in particular the US Congressional committee system) and their ability to deliver stability to an otherwise chaotic legislative environment. Shepsle asserts that committees facilitate a 'structure imposed equilibrium' through both control of the legislative agenda and the tendency towards specialisation. Committees control agendas by the selective emphasis of certain topics, either reporting and making recommendations to the legislature, or conversely 'sitting on' issues that they wish to supress. Specialisation endows a powerful gate-keeping function upon committees, in that modifications to a bill can only deal with matters that are germane to the committee's remit. Shepsle argues that the committee system effectively re-imposes a one-dimensional policy environment upon the legislative game. Key decisions are taken on one dimension at a time and dimensions cannot be linked to one another through trade-offs. Crucially, this also means that the overall package of policies agreed by the legislature will be the aggregate of the policy position of the median legislator on each separate dimension.

Shepsle's model is of enormous significance because it is a formal deductive model of coalition formation which allows for institutional specifics. As such, it has been taken up by other political scientists such as Denzau and Mackay (1987) and Gilligan and Krehbiel (1987), who have looked at the effects on legislative outcomes of other decision rules, such as the amendment procedure. The logic behind all these works is that, whilst theorists may posit the existence of general laws of legislative choice, these are contingent upon a specific 'mix' of facilitators and the constraints on them in each legislature. The existence of institutionally specific decision rules shape actual outcomes, and the winners of the coalition game over time are those that most successfully manipulate the dimensions of such institutions. As Riker puts it, 'in the long run, outcomes are the consequences not only of institutions and tastes, but also of the political skills and artistry of those who manipulate (them) … and just what combination of institutions, tastes and artistry will appear in any given political system is, it seems to me, as unpredictable as poetry. But given the short-term structural and cultural restraints, there is some stability, some predictability of outcomes, and the function of the science of politics is to identify these 'unstable constants' (1980: 445). As will become apparent, it is the 'political skills and artistry' of Gerhard Schröder in particular that have shaped the parameters of the Red–Green model that we are familiar with today.

To sum up, the appeal of Shepsle's model is that it has enabled theorists to factor in the institutional context (as a decision rule), as well as simplifying the concept of policy space. The policy dimension for a given decision game is seen as one dimensional, but it is not restricted to the classic Downsian left–right continuum and can be any form of political dichotomy. The decision space may be between materialist and post-materialist values, between authoritarianism and libertarianism, or between nationalism and internationalism, and so on. The appeal of such an approach is that it not only imposes equilibrium on the model, but that it is consistent with empirical evidence. The reconciliation of deductive reasoning and the institutional context has raised hopes that formal modelling may be more easily applied to the European context, thus bridging the perceived gap between the 'North American' game-theoretical tradition and the more inductive 'European' approach.

As mentioned earlier, two of the most important attempts at this have been in work by Laver and Schofield (1990) and Budge and Keman (1990). Laver and Schofield (1990) build upon Grofman's 'protocoalition' model (1982), as well as Laver's earlier empirical work and argue that, when forming a coalition, parties initially attempt to form a 'protocoalition' with the party nearest them ideologically. Protocoalitions are assumed to then try and grow sufficiently to ensure a winning position within the legislature. This 'bargaining approach' can be either hierarchical (as Grofman originally suggested), or take place in a more rapacious and non-hierarchical manner, whereby protocoalitions form and break up, only to be replaced by another, until the winning post is reached. Laver and Schofield assume that coalition stability and maintenance is the function of three structural attributes, relating to the nature of the regime, the coalition and the bargaining environment.

The authors identify seven 'regime attributes'. First, the gross number of parties in the party system. Second, the net, or 'effective number', of parties in the party system (considered to be more important than the gross number). Third, the presence of anti-system parties. Fourth, the extent of ideological polarisation within the system. Fifth, the level of policy influence open to the opposition through committee scrutiny, etc. Sixth, the degree to which elections are salient to coalition formation, and, finally, the presence (and nature) of a formal investiture requirement. In addition, Laver and Schofield identify three sets of 'coalition attributes': its majority status, its minimal winning status and its minimal connected winning status. They produce data to show that these act as independent variables upon Cabinet duration, and conclude that single-party majority, minimum-winning and ideologically compact coalitions do appear to last longer. They argue that much will depend upon the 'bargaining environment' of a given polity, of which there are three main categories: 'multipolar', 'unipolar' and 'bipolar' systems. Multipolar systems (such as Belgium, Denmark and Italy) are characterised by a complex distribution of party weights and policy positions and, as a result, Cabinets are susceptible to even small changes in such a distribution and are less stable than in other systems. Unipolar systems are either centred (with the dominant party in the political centre) or off-centre (with the dominant party on either the left or right of the political middle ground) and are prone to change, although less so than multipolar systems. Bipolar systems are described as 'simple, clear cut and unchanging' (Laver and Schofield, 1993: 156), in which dramatic shifts are needed to change the underlying bargaining logic of the system (in which almost any two-party coalition is viable). It follows from this that Cabinets are relatively stable because there are few incentives to break up one coalition and form another. The Federal Republic of Germany has traditionally been regarded as a bipolar system, although the question remains whether the German party system will become more akin to the multipolar model (with both the Greens and FDP acting as potential junior coalition partners) or remain bipolar (with the Greens assuming the role of third party at the FDP's expense).

Ultimately, however, Laver and Schofield argue that much will turn upon what they call 'events' and there is a powerful correlation between the predicted stability of coalitions and their actual ability to withstand their impact. They go on to advocate an approach that combines both the 'attributes' and 'events' approach, observing that 'all coalitions, even the most durable, are subject to the potential impact of random events (and) even a very 'durable' government can in practice have quite a short duration if a particularly important event happens to bring down the government early in its potential life' (Laver and Schofield, 1993: 162).

Ian Budge and Hans Keman (1990) aspire to a more formal deductive approach whilst attempting to factor in institutional contexts. They argue that successful coalition formation and maintenance is predicated on a small set of assumptions that can be empirically tested. These are, first, that in parliamentary democracies the party or combination of parties which can win a legislative vote of confidence forms the government. Second, that parties seek to form a government capable of effectively carrying through their declared policy preferences. Third, that the chief preference of all democratic parties is to counter threats to the democratic system but, if no such threats exist, 'socialist-bourgeois' or other 'group-related' differences play a crucial role. Finally, that subject to overall policy agreements and disciplinary and procedural constraints, factions seek to transform their own policy preferences into government policy most effectively (1993: 34). These assumptions are essentially a set of commonsense rules of thumb that would seem reasonable to most observers. However, the third assumption is of particular interest, as it neatly encapsulates the salient issues within the SPD–Green coalition debate. For instance, if democratic parties' first priority is to counter threats to the democratic system, then the perception of the Greens as a potential coalition partner has been contingent upon their attitude to the political norms of the Federal Republic. At first the Greens' attitude towards them was ambiguous and, as a result, they were considered at best an unreliable political partner. But once it was accepted that the Greens were not an anti-democratic party, residual 'socialist-bourgeois' differences became more important. Although this cleavage has become less important in the Federal Republic, it still serves as the primary means of differentiation between left and right. Therefore, to the extent that the Greens are a left-libertarian party, it would follow that political co-oper-ation between them and the SPD could be facilitated along this cleavage.

Nevertheless, it must be remembered that all three conditions are con-tingent upon the perceived conformity to a system of norms, rather than a transparent set of criteria. The concept of a 'democratic' party may apply across cases, but how it is evaluated as a criterion is dependent upon norms that not only vary across space (between different states or regions) but also time (as local conditions change and the political mid-dle-ground shifts). Political scientists need to remain circumspect, even when they aspire to be predictive. Theory is necessary if one is to enhance one's understanding of party systems and political behaviour. But one cannot ignore the specific institutional context or regard the 'political culture' of a given case as static and unchanging. To conclude, the politi-cal scientist must remain aware that even the most elegant model can – and probably will – find itself falsified by the dynamics of practical poli-tics. Given that this is the case, the use of modelling in this book is pri-marily of heuristic value and keeps the institutional context of the Federal Republic at its core.

Using case studies

Chapter 3 gives an account of the history of Red–Green coalitions, from the period of informal co-operation in the early 1980s through to the late 1990s. The logic of the Red–Green model is demonstrated in greater depth in Chapters 4 and 5, which look at the Berlin and Niedersachsen coalitions. In the second half of the book, these are than used as a tem-plate with which to examine the Federal Red–Green coalition.

The use of case studies is intuitively a relatively straightforward idea but some scholars are keen to point out their limitations. For instance, Sartori somewhat obscurely makes the distinction between case studies as a comparative method *per se* and as a method with some merit within the context of a wider comparative analysis (1994: 23). Mackie and Marsh

(1995: 177) have responded to this by accusing Sartori of indulging in pedantry, but one can sympathise with the implicit point that Sartori is making, that case studies alone are a flimsy method of comparison if not informed by a well-defined and operational theoretical framework. This is echoed by Rose, who argues that it is the presence of such an operational framework – capable of application across cases – that makes a study comparative (1991: 449).

Lijphart divides case studies up into five ideal types: first, interpretative case studies using existing theory; second, hypothesis-generating case studies; third, case studies used to interrogate or test a theory; fourth, those used to confirm a theory; fifth, what he calls 'deviant' studies (1971: 691–3). But, as Mackie and Marsh (1995) point out, Lijphart's first category of case study is not strictly comparative anyway and the other four ideal types are not necessarily comparative either. They can only be considered comparative if 'they use and assess the utility of concepts developed elsewhere … to test some general theory or hypothesis, or generate concepts to be of use elsewhere' (1995: 177).

Being ideal types, Lijphart's categories are often not so neatly replicated within the field of comparative research and the use of case studies in this book covers four out of five of the categories (excluding deviant studies). The use of existing models of coalition formation can be regarded as being primarily interpretative rather than comparative, in keeping with Lijphart's first classification, as well as arguably conforming to both the third ('theory informing') and fourth ('theory confirming') ideal types and even the second ('hypothesis-generating') category. The constraints of book length and subject matter have made it necessary to limit the scope of study to two German states. This is in order to prepare the reader for the final part of the book, which examines the politics, policies and personalities that make up the Federal Republic's first Red–Green coalition at the national level. It remains for the reader to judge how successfully the book achieves this.

Theorising Red–Green coalitions

Within the literature, the Federal Republic has traditionally been classified as either a 'two-and-a-half party system' (Blondel, 1968: 112) or a three party system, with a smaller party (normally the liberal FDP) acting as the 'kingmaker' between the two big 'catch-all' parties (Kirchheimer, 1966), the SPD and the Christian Democratic Union (CDU)/Christian Social Union (CSU). This triangular relationship was sustained by the effect of the Federal Republic's Additional Member System (AMS) of proportional representation, which was introduced in 1953. With the exception of a brief period of majority (CDU/CSU) government in the 1950s, over successive legislative periods the AMS system has produced a share of seats in the Bundestag which has made the formation of formal coalitions between the parties a necessity. AMS also produces 'split-ticket' voting, whereby voters divide their allegiance between the first (constituency) and second (party list) votes. Initially, split second votes generally went to the FDP, but in the 1980s the Greens came to benefit from the practice of New Left-oriented SPD voters giving them their second votes.

Because it is relatively proportionate, Germany's system of AMS began to reflect the steady deconcentration of the party system itself. Since the 1970s, this deconcentration has become pronounced, first at the margins then, increasingly, at the core of the electorate. The SPD has been the big loser in this process and, apart from having to compete with the Greens, it has also suffered a severe loss of support amongst its electoral core of Protestants and/or manual workers. Partisan identification for the SPD amongst this group fell 19 per cent during the 1980s (Padgett, 1993a: 38), before recovering slightly in 1994 and 1998 (*Forschungsgruppe Wahlen*, 1990/1994/1998). Since German unification in 1990, party system deconcentration has also been aggravated by the addition of a 'second' party system in the states of the former East Germany, with an 'inverted social profile' of voting behaviour. Although class and confessional classifications are somewhat tentative in Eastern Germany, in the early 1990s the SPD trailed the CDU amongst manual workers as well as all confessional groups (Padgett, 1993: 39-41, and 1995: 87). This trend was reversed somewhat in the 1998 Bundestag election (*Forschungsgruppe Wahlen*, 1998) but the SPD still has to compete for left votes with the successor to old East German SED, the Party of Democratic Socialism (PDS).

From the point of view of the SPD, the proportionality of electoral outcomes provided a 'political opportunity structure' that privileged its left and Green competitors within the legislature. This is replicated at the state-level where electoral rules and party systems are analogous. As a result, the SPD is torn between two conflicting strategic issues: the need for ideological moderation on the one hand and the imperatives of coalition formation on the other. Although the party list system does not enhance the influence of moderate swing voters, in aggregate terms it remains rational for the SPD to adopt the Downsian strategy of the 'median voter'. But having maximised the SPD vote on election day, the rules of the game change considerably. Unless it has done exceptionally well and achieved an overall majority within a given legislature, the SPD has to form a coalition with one or more of the other parties if it is to get past the minimal winning post of 50 per cent plus one seat. But in order to do this, all parties have to be confident that co-operation is possible. The choice of coalition partner carries an extra risk for the SPD, because of the principle of Ministerial autonomy (the *Ressortsprinzip*) which is protected in the Federal Republic's Basic Law. In both quantitative and qualitative terms, the distribution of Ministerial seats between the parties is central to the coalition bargaining process and, once a formal agreement has been signed, it is hard to rectify mistakes. Given the tendency of parties to staff Ministries with their own people, policy making can become a vehicle for inter-coalition rivalry. Thus, policy-specific sub-committees set up during coalition negotiations become the key gate-keepers within the process: not just in terms of the allocation of specific portfolios but also in setting the parameters of policy areas and the terms of reference between them. Coalition bargaining is a potentially fraught process and building on the theoretical models described earlier in this chapter I suggest that the following set of assumptions underpin the parties' calculations.

First, given that all parties possess policy-related preferences, it is logical that they will desire to be a member of the coalition that is closest to them in policy terms. Ideally, such a coalition will be connected and will have the least ideological range, within which each party will hope to be in the median position along the relevant (Downsian left–right and/or 'materialist/post-materialist') policy dimension. It is assumed that these positions are the aggregate of each policy sector taken separately, in other words multiple one-dimensional policy sectors. This is in the tradition of Kenneth Shepsle's concept of a 'structure induced equilibrium', except that the gate-keeper is the sub-committee for each policy sector within the overall coalition negotiations. All parties want to be in the median position along a policy dimension in order to minimise the ideological range of the coalition in relation to its preferred position. It is also assumed that parties are aware that the larger a coalition's ideological range, the more potential for disagreement over policy, and that large majorities tend to be more unstable than minimal-winning ones. In addition, they might accept Axelrod's common-sense proposition that the more partners there are in a coalition, the more potential exists for conflicts of interest.

If these assumptions are correct, when Red–Green coalitions form it is because they are the minimal connected winning coalition with the smallest 'ideological range' (de Swaan, 1973), but – as this book demonstrates – the factors determining their success are more complex and nuanced. In this book I suggest that the process of political co-operation between the SPD and Greens has, over time, led to the formulation of an 'ideal type' or 'Red–Green model' (Lees, 1999) which has developed over time. Drawing upon the institutional knowledge acquired during the period of co-operation at the sub-national level, the question of successful coalition formation and maintenance hinges upon three sets of issues. It will become clear that this 'ideal type' draws upon both positive and negative lessons and the discounting of unsuccessful alternative arrangements (such as the informal arrangements in Hamburg in 1982 and the ill-starred 'Traffic Light' coalitions of the early 1990s in Brandenburg and Bremen).

The first 'bundle' of issues relates to the parties' ideological stance and election programmes. For the SPD, this meant that the selective emphasis of the post-materialist and/or libertarian dimension – that is, 'quality of life' issues – has been a prerequisite of successful co-operation with the Greens. For their part, the Greens have found that working with the SPD has required a moderation of the more post-materialist and/or libertarian side of their ideological profile, and in particular their ambivalence to consumer capitalism, the state's monopoly on legitimate force and its external defence arrangements. The second bundle of issues relates to the composition and division of portfolios, codified in a formal coalition agreement. It became clear very quickly that a formal coalition agreement was required if any degree of stability was to be established. Moreover, the lessons of the past meant that the SPD regarded ownership of certain 'core' or 'sensitive' portfolios (particularly the Finance, Economics and Industry Ministries) as the benchmark of co-operation with the Greens. The Greens would learn through bitter experience that future Red–Green coalitions would not be possible without their owning the Environment portfolio, preferably with both the Ministerial and State Secretary posts, whilst avoiding the creation of 'super-Ministries' as part of the coalition horse trading. Finally, the staffing and structure of the civil service and the wider issue of expertise were sensitive areas for the Greens. Their coalition partners the SPD were 'expertise rich', which meant that, when they took over a Ministry, existing staff could be replaced from in-house if so desired. This reduced the start-up costs to the SPD when taking office, leading to continuity of policy making and the retention of institutional knowledge. It had the effect of a 'virtuous circle' in that such expertise filtered back into the party networks, informing their policy-making discourse and educating a future cadre. All in all, it meant that the reform of the policy-making apparatus was generally quite low down the SPD's agenda. By contrast, the Greens were 'expertise poor', with very few in-house resources to call upon when taking over a Ministry and precious little experience within the party networks. For the Greens it was crucial that they open up the existing policy network to their client groups, in order not only to get access to their expertise but, over time, to train their own personnel. Significantly, it would also serve to demonstrate to their own supporters that not only was the 'Long March through the Länder' over, but that it had been worth it.

3

The long march through the Länder

The SPD and the challenge of the Greens

The SPD is the oldest political party in the Federal Republic and its origins date back to the failed revolutionary fervour of 1848. Its roots are deeply embedded in the network of workers' clubs that spread throughout the more industrialised regions of Germany in the latter half of the nineteenth century. The emergent party was polarised between two competing socialist groups, the Lassalleans and the Eisenachers. This polarisation manifested itself not only in their political outlook, but also in their formal organisation. The effect of this division between the two groups has persisted until the present. As Hunt observes, the two groups 'left a strange dual heritage to the later party, which helps to explain some of its paradoxes' (1964: 2).

The SPD has always had an authoritarian streak, dating back to one of its precursors, the German General Workers Association (*Allgemeiner Deutscher Arbeitervereien* or ADA), founded in the mid nineteeneth century by Lassalle. Lassalle declared in a letter to Bismarck 'that the working classes are instinctively inclined to dictatorship, if they can be justly convinced that this dictatorship is exercised in their interests' (Hunt, 1964: 4). As Hunt observes, 'from its outset the German labour movement has a dual heritage in organisational as well as in political matters … two sharply contrasting models of organisation: the one authoritarian, rigidly centralised, efficient, and disciplined, the other ultra-democratic, loosely federalist in structure, and lax in discipline. In the subsequent history of the SDP, one can follow the interplay of these two clashing concepts of organisation' (Hunt, 1964: 6–7).

The story of the modern SPD begins with the defeat of Hitler in 1945. At first, the SPD was able to remobilise under the aegis of all the occupying powers. But following a forced merger with the Communist Party of

Germany (KPD) in the Russian zone in the spring of 1946, the SPD's activities were restricted to the three Western zones of occupation. The SPD at this time remained in many respects a Marxist-inspired party of the non-communist left. It took a long time to come to terms with the post-war settlement, the division of Germany and the 'social market economy' model being developed by Adenauer and Erhard, with the encouragement of the Americans. The post-war SPD's early policy pronouncements continued to promise to 'socialise' the production of coal, iron and steel, energy, chemicals, basic building materials, large banks and insurance companies. Such a stance set the SPD against the political tide in the Western zones. Following election defeats in 1949, 1953 and 1957, the SPD began to modify its electoral stance. The process of adapting to the new political realities of the Federal Republic culminated in the Bad Godesberg conference of 1959, when the party adopted a new raft of policies. The 'Bad Godesberg Programme' disavowed Marxism and attempted to embed the SPD's core principles of democratic socialism within the wider context of Christian ethics, classical philosophy and the tradition of humanism. The programme endorsed the liberal pluralist settlement in the Federal Republic and the centrality of the social market economy to it.

Underlying this change was the need to appeal across class loyalties in order to enhance the SPD's support. This logic of the 'Völkspartei' predated Kirchheimer's (1966) model of the 'catch-all' party which explicitly de-emphasises ideology and class allegiance as a means of political mobilisation. Combined with a new professional team led by the charismatic Willy Brandt, the party's new moderate stance led to a ten point rise in SPD support over the period 1957–69. Finally, in 1972, the SPD reached the peak of their popularity: polling 45.8 per cent of the vote and becoming the biggest party in the Bundestag (Padgett, 1993a: 28). The SPD's new moderation and rising electoral support inevitably led to participation in national government, first as junior partner to the Christian Democratic CDU in the Grand Coalition of 1966–69, and then as senior partner to the liberal FDP in the Social–Liberal Coalition of 1969–82. But ever since its peak of popularity in 1972, the SPD has been in both an electoral and ideological decline. This decline accelerated in the 1980s, following the collapse of the Social–Liberal coalition.

Once in opposition, the SPD had to respond to four fundamental threats to its position. First, the decline in the overall vote for the two 'catch-all' parties, which has effected both the SPD and CDU, and has prompted some observers to forecast growing instability within the Federal Republic's party system. Second, the extraordinary personal appeal and political acumen of Helmut Kohl, who has managed to keep the SPD on the back foot in the fight for the political centre ground. Third, the growth of the Greens, which has served to put pressure on the SPD along the post-materialist or 'New Politics' dimension. Finally, after 1990, the persistence of the PDS in the new Eastern states, which has contributed to the SPD's weakness in the East and (with the additional weakness of the Greens and FDP) has severely restricted their coalition options. At the state level, the SPD has continued to thrive as a party of government. From the early 1980s onwards, the SPD began to embark upon a strategy of co-operation with emergent Green party. Over time, the Greens evolved into a party that the SPD could work with, as demonstrated by 'Red–Green' coalitions in, for example, the states of Hessen (1985–87, 1991–95 and 1995–99), West Berlin (1989–90), Niedersachsen (1990–94) and Nordrhein-Westfalen (1995–) as well as the minority coalition ('tolerated' by the PDS) in Saxony-Anhalt between 1994 and 1998. In addition there have been 'Traffic-Light' coalitions in Brandenburg between 1990 and 1994 (with Alliance 1990 and the FDP) and Bremen between 1991 and 1995 (with the Greens and the FDP).

The Greens come in from the cold

The Greens had emerged out of the 'citizens initiative' groups of the mid to late 1970s. The early years were characterised by internecine struggle between the ecology movement's 'New Left' and conservative wings. The former saw environmental protest as one aspect of a wider critique of the capitalist system (and were more prepared to resort to violent political protest against it), whilst the latter favoured co-operation with the established political order. As a result, the two wings began to field rival lists at local and Länder elections. However, it was clear that such factionalism was preventing either of the ecological groupings from surmounting the Federal Republic's 5 per cent electoral barrier and, in July 1978, the two wings in Bayern decided to combine and take part in the state's elections, due in October of that year. This arrangement became known as the 'Bayern Co-operation Model' and became the template for future co-operation in other states. Once inside the same organisation, the conservative elements became progressively marginalised and the new party began to assume its familiar left-libertarian and/or post-materialist character (Markovits and Gorski, 1993: 192–7).

The Greens' first opportunities came at the local level, where they took advantage of the greater willingness of voters to vote innovatively at local elections (as well as the fact that many local communities had no 5 per cent electoral barrier). They also campaigned in the 1979 elections to the European Parliament and, although failing to win seats, the various fractured Green groupings in the Federal Republic did win a respectable 3.2 per cent of the vote. While many local Green parties formed during this period, others did not contest local elections until after the formation of the national party in 1980. Thus the formative experiences of local Green parties did not always follow a set pattern, resulting in quite heterogeneous local political cultures that persisted into the 1990s.

The big breakthrough for the Greens came in March 1983, when the national party entered the Bundestag for the first time, having won 5.6 per cent of the vote in national elections (Padgett, 1993a: 28). Klaus von Beyme asserts that 'the 1983 election transformed the Federal Republic from the last refuge of party system immobility into an El Dorado of success for alternative politics' (1991: 161). This may be over-stating the case a little, but it is clear that from that point onwards the German party system was undergoing a process of change and adaptation.

Over time, six factors have been at work which have served to bring the Greens into the political mainstream. First, following unification, the merger of the more moderate Alliance '90 and 'Eastern' Greens with the Greens in the 'old' Federal Republic has resulted in an overall moderation of both the Green voters' and membership's ideological profile. Second, the original generational cohort from which the movement in the West originally arose has got older, become more established and integrated. Third, as the Greens have become more established within the political system, their internal structure has become more institutionalised and hierarchical. Fourth, the agenda around which the Greens have mobilised has been co-opted by the other parties – especially the SPD – in a process that became known as 'theme theft' (*Themenklau*). Fifth, the increasing failure of the FDP to pass the 5 per cent barrier in the states, and its reliance at both the local and national level upon the second-votes of CDU supporters, has increased the viability (and therefore the desirability) of the Greens as a potential coalition partner. Finally, the survival and persistence of the post-communist PDS after unification in 1990 has meant that much of the stigma that had previously attached itself to the Greens (especially during the cold war) has now been transferred to them. Thus, there is less political risk in other parties co-operating with the Greens.

As a result, the Greens can now be regarded as a party of the mainstream at the sub-national level. That the Greens have both stabilised their vote share and become an established feature of the party system may have surprised some observers but is not without precedent. Indeed, the SPD itself underwent the same process earlier this century (see Padgett, 1993b). Nevertheless, what is striking is the speed with which this process has taken place, despite the Greens' lack of a clear social cleavage around which to mobilise. This has led some observers to wonder if a 'post-industrial' cleavage now exists or, alternatively, that cleavage structures are no longer relevant to the modern German party system (see Raschke, 1993).

It would still be rash to deny the persistence of the old materialist social-political divisions or to speculate as to their continuing salience in the future. The German party system has adapted to accommodate the Greens rather than been transformed by them. Conversely, whilst the two big catch-all parties have seen some slippage in their vote, they remain the major players within the party system and the Greens have had to deal with this fact.

Red–Green political co-operation: learning the art of compromise

The history of political co-operation between the SPD and the Greens has been one of trial and error. From the vantage point of the start of the twenty-first century, it is easy to forget that the earliest Red–Green experiments often provided a bumpy political ride for all concerned. Since then, it has been a process of learning, with co-operation becoming progressively easier over time. The learning curve has become ever steeper as the Greens assumed a more formal and hierarchical party structure. As a result, local Green party organisations have become less particularist and more homogenised, their ideological profile more moderate and their strategic behaviour more predictable.

The first example of Red–Green political co-operation took place in the Hanseatic city-state of Hamburg. The June 1982 elections to the Hamburg parliament yielded two mathematically feasible coalition outcomes, in both of which the SPD had to be represented. These were either a 'Grand Coalition' of the SPD and CDU, or some form of agreement between the SPD and the local 'Grüne Alternative Liste' (GAL). At this time, the Hamburg GAL was a stronghold of the hardline 'fundi' tendency and, as such, was not altogether well-disposed towards the SPD. But the local party was put under a great deal of pressure by other local Green parties to come to a deal with the Social Democrats. The GAL refused to consider a coalition with the SPD, but agreed to a degree of co-operation on condition that the Social Democrats met certain key requirements.[1] Although the SPD were split over the GAL's demands, they agreed to enter into dialogue with the Greens in order to secure their political support. After the GAL helped defeat a no confidence motion tabled by the local CDU, the Social Democrats invited them into formal negotiations. This first tentative move by the Hamburg SPD was greeted with dismay by both the national leadership – in the form of Chancellor Helmut Schmidt – and other state-level leaders, most notably the Minister President of Hessen, Holger Börner, who was deeply critical of Hamburg Mayor, Klaus von Dohnanyi.

There then followed a period of successive ups and downs in the climate of co-operation between the two parties. At first, the mood lifted as the GAL co-operated in passing a bridging credit authorisation in order to keep the city government functioning. But the political weather deteriorated following the involvement of a GAL leader in a squatting action, at a time when the Social Democrats were clearing squatted houses. This was followed by the GAL parliamentary faction tabling a proposal to declare Hamburg a nuclear-free zone. With no progress on the original demands of the GAL, the SPD called new elections to try and break the impasse. With a total of 196 days, it had been the shortest legislative period in the history of the Hamburg parliament! The new elections yielded an absolute majority for the SPD, although, as Markovits and Gorski point out, the Social Democrats' gains were almost entirely at the expense of the CDU and FDP, rather than the GAL who polled almost 7 per cent of the vote (Markovits and Gorski, 1993: 202).

The Hamburg experience highlighted two elements that were to become part of the pattern of Red–Green co-operation. First, that the prospect of co-operation exposed the internal divisions within the two parties. In the Hamburg case, the GAL was broadly 'fundi' in its outlook and was able to mobilise around a fairly unyielding strategic position. The local SPD was split between the traditional right, who were opposed to co-operation with the GAL, and the party's 'New Left' tendency, who were often – for example regarding the proposal to declare Hamburg a nuclear-free zone – more in agreement with the GAL than with their own leadership. In other instances it was to be the Greens who were split and the SPD who were able to exploit such divisions. The second element was that the strategic decisions taken by the two parties during such a process of co-operation had subsequent electoral consequences. For instance, in the Hamburg case both parties ultimately took a hard line with the other. This seems to have had the effect of enhancing the SPD's electoral support at the expense of the other mainstream parties whilst, at the same time, limiting that of the GAL (who had expected to improve on their previous showing).

Subsequent examples of SPD–Green co-operation seem to support the impression that, outside of their hard-core 'milieu', a great deal of the Greens' electoral support is contingent upon them co-operating with the SPD and that an explicitly fundamentalist stance is punished by the voters. On the other hand, the SPD appears to benefit from taking a firm stance with the Greens. Conversely, where the SPD has been seen to tack too far to the left, it has tended to alienate its core blue-collar voters.

With the SPD majority in the Hamburg parliament securely ensconced for the legislative period, attention shifted to the south-western state of Hessen. Although not a 'heartland' in the sense of the blue-collar industrial state of Nordrhein-Westfalen, Hessen was one of the 'reddest' of the German states. However the left tradition in Hessen was relatively heterogeneous, with old left strongholds in the big cities being balanced by a New Left influence in the University towns such as Marburg, as well as in the south of the state. It is not surprising, therefore, that many of the most salient developments in the Red–Green model of political co-operation took place – and indeed continue to take place – within that state's party system. Nevertheless, in the early 1980s, conditions in Hessen were such that the prospects for Red–Green political co-operation were not at all auspicious, with a number of powerful local SPD politicians deeply opposed to co-operation with the Greens. The most important of these at that time was Minister President Holger Börner.

As already mentioned, it was Börner who had publicly opposed Klaus von Dohnanyi's early efforts to forge an alliance with the Hamburg GAL. Not surprisingly, Börner's antipathy extended to the Hessen Greens, despite the fact that they were widely recognised as being one of the more moderate of the Green parties in the German states. That was not to say that there were no grounds for mistrust between the two parties. In particular, violent disorder associated with the ecology groups' opposition to the building of a new runway at Frankfurt International Airport[2] was an ongoing source of tension between the two parties in the state.

The Hessen state parliament elections of 26 September 1982 presented the SPD and the Greens with the mathematical possibility of a Red–Green coalition. As a result, Börner found himself presented with a dilemma. Not only did he personally oppose co-operation with the Greens, but he had made promises during the election to that effect. He was now forced to reconsider his position. Within a month of the elec-

tions, Börner had recanted enough to ensure Green support for his candidature as 'chief parliamentary executive', pending planned new elections in the Autumn of 1983. In the meantime, the Hessen Greens
supported an SPD initiative to tackle unemployment in the state. This
represented the first instance in the history of the Federal Republic in
which SPD legislation had been passed with the help of the Greens,
although this again fell short of a formal coalition arrangement.

This new spirit of co-operation soon fell foul of politicking. For their
part, the Greens attempted to up the ante and refused to pass the SPD's
budget in the form it was presented to the state parliament. With one eye
on the recent success of the Hamburg SPD's tough stance in relation to
the Greens, Börner called new elections earlier than planned. Subsequently, the SPD's campaign was sharply worded against the Greens,
although – under pressure from New Left delegates – the state party
refused to rule out the possibility of co-operation with the Greens. This
was just as well, as the new parliamentary arithmetic still precluded the
SPD's return to office without the assistance of the Greens.

Again, the process by which the two parties came to formalise a strategy of co-operation was difficult. The Greens initially took the initiative,
offering what they called 'continual co-operation' with the Social
Democrats. This was reciprocated by the SPD, with Börner himself making a speech at the SPD's party congress in which he stated the historical
nature of the negotiations with the Greens. With the CDU/CSU and FDP
newly elected to government in Bonn, Börner recognised that Hessenn's
Red–Green model would provide a much-needed political counter-
weight (Markovits and Gorski, 1993: 206). It was agreed that the Greens
would support the SPD in passing the 1983 and 1984 budgets.

The euphoria was short-lived, however, as resistance surfaced in both
parties. At the beginning of 1984, the Greens informed the SPD that their
support in passing that year's budget was contingent upon the SPD agree-
ing to a new set of demands. This was an attempt to move the political
agenda on from what was essentially a holding pattern, designed to keep
the CDU out of office, to something nearer the 'new politics' that the
Greens wished to promote. Börner gave assurances to the Greens and, in
the June of 1984, the Hessen SPD's party congress approved continued
co-operation. But there were growing signs of dissent in the SPD ranks.
This dissent was given added momentum in the October of 1984, when a
Green party congress passed a motion that made further co-operation
contingent upon the SPD's cancellation of an extension of the local
NUKEM nuclear power plant and of an order for weapons grade pluto-

nium from ALKEM, another plant in the state. The SPD's right-wing were outraged.

To allow these demands to become entrenched as the benchmark of Red–Green co-operation would have meant the end of the experiment. For those within the two parties who remained well-disposed towards further co-operation – mainly the SPD's New Left and the moderate 'realo' wing of the Greens – it was clear that the process had to be moved on to a more formal footing. In particular, the 'realos' had to be able to have something to show as a result of such co-operation, if they were to counter the criticism from the 'fundi' wing. For the committed 'fundis', by definition all co-operation with the SPD was bad in itself. The crucial battle was for the party's grass roots membership, who were amenable to co-operation if it brought results, but anxious that basic Green principles were not sold short. Ordinary members needed to be convinced that working with the SPD would enhance the Greens' influence upon events.

Throughout the winter of 1984–85, activists on both sides pushed for a formal coalition agreement to be signed between the two parties and, in May 1985, Börner formally offered such an arrangement. In return for entering into a coalition with the SPD, the Greens would get the Ministry for Environment and Energy. The price would be that the Greens would not be able to further hold the SPD to ransom over passing the budget. Not only would the 1985 budget have to be passed, but also a 'double budget' for 1986–87. The Greens rejected the double budget idea and the 'fundis' demanded two Ministries, including a Ministry for Women. The final deal represented a compromise between the two positions. The Greens resisted the commitment to pass the budgets and insisted on two separate budget processes, although the SPD insisted that these processes be capped and last no more than a year. For its part, the SPD resisted the creation of a Ministry for Women, but the Greens were able to appoint an advisor on Women's issues within the Ministry of Health, Family and Education. But the bottom line was control of the Ministry for Environment and Energy. Local Green 'realo', Joschka Fischer, became the party's first state-level Environment Minister, and the Greens formally entered sub-national government for the first time.

The subsequent Red–Green coalition of 1985–87 (and to a lesser extent its successor of 1991–95, which was re-elected in February 1995) in Hessen is considered by many to be the template for such coalitions, both in other states and to some extent at the national level. It is certainly the most documented (Scharf, 1994, Markovits and Gorski, 1993, Padgett, 1993a, Kleinert, 1992, Hülsberg, 1988). One reason for this has been Hessen's strong 'realo' tradition, which has meant that local politicians such as Joschka Fischer have also been leading figures nationally. Moreover Hessen's 5 per cent electoral barrier makes it an analogue of the national system as a whole: making comparison with the national level easier. But the main reasons for the importance of the Hessen experience has been threefold. It was the first formed at state level, it has since been the longest lasting and is the first to have been re-elected.

The 'Red–Green experiment' (as it was branded by its critics) of 1985–87 is best remembered for Joschka Fischer's tenure as the first Green Minister for the Environment. It is a good example of both the facilitating and constraining nature of the German policy-making process. As already mentioned, Fischer was firmly on the 'realo' wing of the party and this was reflected in his strategy of concentrating on the stricter implementation of existing legislation (*nach Gesetz und Recht*). In this he was quite successful. For instance, with regard to the chemical industry, he forced companies (in particular Hoechst AG) to install new instrumentation in order to meet lower permitted limits of industrial discharges into the River Main. Given the sheer economic and political clout wielded by the Hoechst concern in the state of Hessen, the success of Fischer's Ministry in enforcing these changes had a seismic impact upon future expectations.

The late 1980s was a period of hope for the Greens and those in the SPD who regarded the Red–Green model as a viable option. The Chernobyl disaster of 1986 had pushed the environment to the forefront of the political agenda, resulting in the establishment of the Federal Ministry for Environment, Nature Protection and Reactor Safety. Given this context, the state elections in Niedersachsen in the June of 1986 presented a fresh opportunity. Prior to the elections, the SPD leader, Gerhard Schröder, had declared himself amenable to overtures from the Greens whilst, for their part, the local Greens made an unconditional offer of coalition negotiations to the SPD before a single vote had been cast. If a Red–Green coalition were formed, it was widely expected that this would put the CDU/CSU–FDP coalition in Bonn under pressure in the run-up to the Federal elections scheduled for 25 January 1987. As it turned out, nothing of the sort was to happen. The CDU–FDP coalition in Hannover was returned with a slim majority and the CDU/CSU–FDP would be returned to Bonn the following year. But the feeling remained that the Red–Green model was an idea whose time was coming.

Ironically, whilst the Chernobyl disaster brought environmental concerns into the political mainstream, within the Greens it enhanced the credibility of the 'fundi' left. This led to another bout of internal party feuding, given added bitterness by the collapse of the Hessen coalition, the failures of the Niedersachsen and Federal elections and subsequent set-backs in the elections in Hamburg and the Rheinland-Pfalz in May 1987, and Bremen and Schleswig-Holstein in September 1987.

This bout of internecine blood-letting was to end with the creation of the centrist 'Aufbruch' group in the January of 1988, heralding the eventual demise of the 'fundi' wing. But the road ahead was still rocky. In March 1988, hopes were raised when the Baden-Württemberg Greens scored almost 8 per cent of the vote, but two months later their Schleswig-Holstein colleagues again failed to surmount the 5 per cent barrier. It was not until after the West Berlin elections of January 1989 that the SPD and Greens seized the opportunity once more to co-operate. The following year, in May 1990, elections in Niedersachsen made another Red–Green coalition possible and, for a few months, there was once more talk of such an arrangement in Bonn, if the legislative arithmetic allowed. Again, this was not to be.

The same year a variation of the model – the 'Traffic Light' coalition (with the FDP as a third partner) – came to power in the new state of Brandenburg. The following year, electoral reverses for the SPD in Bremen led to the same arrangement there. By 1995, neither of these coalitions remained in place. The Brandenburg coalition collapsed early in 1994, after defections from the Greens, demonstrating that the presence of the economically liberal FDP within such a coalition puts great strain upon the process of coalition maintenance and an even greater strain upon party management within the Greens. This is because the inevitable concessions to economic liberalism associated with such coalitions are just too much for many Greens, especially a significant proportion of the party's grass roots membership. Similarly, the Bremen coalition collapsed in January 1995, forcing the state elections to be brought forward from the Autumn to May 1995. Again, the presence of the FDP proved too much for coalition management. However, the defections in Bremen came primarily from the SPD's right-wing, who objected to the party making too many concessions to the Greens.[3] Nevertheless, by the Bundestag election year of 1998, there were four Red–Green coalitions in place in the German states. These were in Hessen, Saxony-Anhalt (tolerated by the PDS), Nordrhein-Westfalen and Schleswig-Holstein. All four coalitions had, at some point, been lauded as the model for a future coalition in Bonn. But their records in office were mixed.

In Hessen, the SPD and Greens had returned to government following state elections in 1991. The coalition ruled successfully for a full term and was re-elected in February 1995. As such, it was the first Red–Green coalition to be voted back into office. But within a matter of months, the Hessen Greens suffered a massive collapse in morale. Even though the coalition remained reasonably popular with the voters, the Green parliamentary faction in the state capital of Wiesbaden was perceived as being out of touch with the grass roots, bereft of ideas and accident prone. The problems of the Hessen Greens could, arguably, be directly or indirectly blamed on the decision of local political godfather, Joschka Fischer, to move to Bonn and become the Greens' parliamentary faction leader in the Bundestag. The move to Bonn meant that the local party was denied his undoubted political skills and there was no obvious successor. Moreover, the two Green Ministers in the coalition were perceived to have been ineffective.

Finally, in March 1999, the Red–Green coalition in Hessen was voted out of office. On leaving office, out-going SPD Minister President Hans Eichel, made it clear that he blamed this setback on the unpopularity of the national Red–Green government. But it was clear that the local coalition had been in political trouble for some time. The Hessen Greens' troubles are essentially two-fold. First, they had become very much like the other political parties in both style and substance, which had led to disillusionment amongst young voters. As one young academic put it, 'the automatic impulse to vote Green is broken'. Although the majority of Green voters remained true to the party, the PDS was able to mobilise support at the margins of the Greens' core support. This tendency was not helped by Fischer's insistence that the Hessen Greens take over the 'classical' Ministerial portfolio of Justice. This may have made sense in terms of demonstrating the Greens ability to govern, but did not play well with the party's grass roots. Despite the fact that the Justice portfolio was taken by Rupert von Plottnitz (whose credentials as a former lawyer for the Red Army Faction seemed ideal for the job), the Ministry was perceived as not being an appropriate area for a Green politician to take an interest. This was despite a commitment in the coalition agreement to undertake a programme of reforms, including the reduction of state surveillance of citizens, data-protection measures, increased use of non-custodial sentences, and so on.

The second reason for Greens' political troubles was that the trade-off for getting the Justice Ministry meant that the Greens had to accept the creation of a 'super-Ministry' for the Environment, Energy, Health, Youth and the Family. This exposed Minister Iris Baul to conflicting political demands that proved desperately hard to reconcile. On the one hand, the 'post-materialist' agenda of environmental protection placed a premium on a critique of existing biases towards production and consumption. On the other, whilst an explicitly Green policy for health, youth and the family could be envisaged, these policy areas have always been the domain of statist and production/consumption-oriented solutions where the emphasis has been on delivery systems to address specific problems, rather than through the adoption of a holistic approach. Iris Baul was faced with trying to reconcile these demands. In addition to this strategic problem, Frau Baul never managed to establish a working relationship with her State Secretary. She resigned as early as September 1995.

The record of the 1995–99 Hessen coalition was not all bad. On the plus side of the ledger, internal disputes were kept to a minimum and the coalition undertook a thorough shake-up of the personnel and structure of the state's administration. But taken as a whole, the overwhelming impression was one of scandals and policy drift.

The Saxony-Anhalt coalition's inauguration was overshadowed by the so-called 'red socks' scandal. The state elections of June 1994 had led to the PDS being the third biggest party in the legislature, after the CDU (with 34.4 per cent of the vote) and the SPD (just behind with 34.0 per cent of the vote). Although not acceptable as a coalition partner, the PDS 'tolerated' the establishment of a minority SPD–Green coalition in the state parliament. Ironically, given the opprobrium that all the 'Western' mainstream parties have attached to the PDS, it was the national leadership of the SPD in Bonn who pressured the reluctant local party into a minority coalition with the Greens. In the context of the run-up to the 1994 Bundestag elections, it gave the CDU an opportunity to play on the fears and prejudices of the voters (Lees, 1995).[4] Despite the scandal, the coalition was one of the most pragmatic on record. Because the Greens are so weak in the Eastern states, they were unwilling to rock the boat. With the PDS's approval, SPD Minister President Reinhard Höppner, was able to push through measures, such as planning permission for a new motorway through the Harz mountains, that were distinctly 'ungreen' and growth oriented in their conception.

The Nordrhein-Westfalen coalition has been an embarrassment for many Social Democrats. The state has traditionally been the SPD's heartland throughout the post-war period. Indeed, from 1980 until the state elections of May 1995, they had governed alone. SPD Minister President Johannes Rau, had been in office since 1979 and was entrenched as the 'father of the state' and, in the run-up to the elections, all the polls indicated that the SPD would again be returned with an absolute majority. Therefore, the results of the 1985 elections were a grave disappointment for the SPD and for Rau personally, who had campaigned on a 'strong government' ticket that precluded negotiating with the Greens. The SPD suffered a massive loss of support (almost 500,000 votes compared with the previous election) amongst its core electorate. At the same time, the Greens made impressive gains, for instance polling almost 30 per cent in one inner-city constituency of Cologne (Green, 1995: 155). Since 1995, the SPD and Greens have governed together with little real enthusiasm for the project. The local SPD is faction ridden, and both Rau and his successor Wolfgang Clement have found it difficult to keep the coalition together.

In many ways, the Red–Green coalition regarded as the best model for the future Bonn government has been in Schleswig-Holstein. This is ironic, because in the 1980s the local Greens had a reputation for fundamentalism. Despite this the coalition has been characterised by a cordial working relationship between SPD Minister President Heidi Simonis and her Green counterpart, Environment Minister Rainder Steenblok, despite the fact that Simonis was on the record prior to the election as favouring an alliance with the FDP. Some of this harmony dissipated in the run-up to the coalition's successful re-election in February 2000, but party management remains the key to its success. Earlier in the life of the coalition, even the opposition paid a grudging tribute to its record, with CDU parliamentary faction leader Martin Kayenburg admitting that 'the [Red–Green] chaos had not shown itself in government' (*Focus*, 23 June 1997).

Constraints on policy making

Throughout the 1980s and into the 1990s, the Greens' status as a relatively new party – and its hostility to traditional rational legal discourses of the policy-making establishment – caused them problems when dealing with the civil service in states in which they governed. Despite his high profile role in Hessen, Joschka Fischer encountered staffing problems within his new Ministry and was forced to appeal to the Administrative Court in Wiesbaden in order to be granted permission to establish a hypothecated personnel advisory board to side step the existing (SPD-dominated) boards (Grant, Paterson and Whitson, 1988: 253–5). The problem of staffing of Green Ministries is not a problem that has been confined to the Hessen coalition. The Federal Republic's policy-making environment is characterised by the penetration of the civil service by the mainstream political parties, who placed appointees at all levels of the administration. At the same time, this resulted in the reciprocal effect whereby the political parties' own ideological profile was shaped by the technocratic discourse of the civil service. With regard to the SPD, this resulted in the moderation of what had traditionally been a Marxist-informed ideological stance in favour of a technocratic administrative/welfarist orientation. This was particularly the case in those states – such as Nordrhein-Westfalen and Berlin – where the Social Democrats had been the dominant party. Thus, by the 1970s, the SPD – and indeed the trade unions – were dominated by the same growth-oriented, welfarist consensus as the CDU/CSU and the FDP (with the exception of its neo-liberal wing). This consensus extended beyond elected politicians to all levels of public administration.

This has presented the Greens with a four-fold problem. First, the fusion presents problems to any new political competitor, regardless of ideological profile, to break into what is essentially an 'iron triangle' between parties, administrators and producer/consumer groups, once that iron triangle has achieved a stable equilibrium. In other words, the fusion raises the opportunity costs of entry into the political/policy-making nexus. Second, as an explicitly left-libertarian and/or post-materialist party, the Greens were particularly hindered by the existence of such a growth-oriented cross-party consensus, operating not only at the political level, but also at the policy-making level. The potential for institutional resistance to explicitly 'Green' policies in such an environment is obvious, especially if the (in)action of civil servants is informed not only by scepticism towards unfamiliar policy objectives, but also by partisan interests. A third problem is that, having identified civil servants who were potentially obstructive, if these civil servants were also members of the SPD they were harder to transfer or retire, because they were, on paper at least, political allies. If the civil servant was high ranking, such as a State Secretary, the problem was especially acute. Not only would such an administrator have a relatively high status and political profile – making him/her harder to get rid of anyway – but they were also often in a position to protect other resistors lower down the hierarchy of the Ministry. Finally, even if all the other problems were overcome, the Greens still needed to find sympathetic administrators of sufficient calibre to take over from the old hands.

One solution was to identify such people from within the administration but, given that most organisations are inherently conservative, there were no guarantees that sufficient numbers of such free-thinkers could be found. The alternative was to 'parachute in' expertise from within the ranks of the Greens. The danger with this was that, even if they were brilliant within their field, they might not be familiar with the dark arts of bureaucratic in-fighting, especially if this was against entrenched institutional resistors. Ideally, they needed to find expertise that was sufficiently outwith the civil service consensus to be amenable to programmatic innovation. If these people came from a non-civil service background, they needed to be serious people, preferably with some experience of dealing with hierarchies and relatively closed policy networks. Inevitably, or worryingly, depending on one's point of view, many of these individuals were to be found within academia! This was especially the case in Berlin, which not only benefited from a large university community, but was also host to numerous environmental consultancies and lobbyists for sources of renewable energy such as solar power. This deep resource base of environmental expertise was enhanced by the presence of the Federal Environment Agency (*Umweltbundesamt*) in Berlin. But this wealth of external expertise is not replicated across the Federal Republic to the same degree, and many Green appointees have been blocked by hostile officialdom, often SPD affiliated. Not surprisingly, the Greens' mixed experience in government has made them more suspicious of administrative hierarchy than ever. In Hessen, the structure of administration was reformed during the mid 1990s and Greens in other states have considered doing the same (Lees, 1998). Nevertheless, it remains to be seen if similar reforms can be easily introduced at the Federal level.

Notes

1 Including the enaction of an emergency programme to combat the state's rising unemployment, the reversal of all budgetary austerity measures and an exit from the use of atomic energy (*Kernenergieausstieg*).
2 Startbahn West was the planned new western runway of Frankfurt international airport. Throughout the early 1980s, this development was the focus of a bitter and violent campaign of attrition between the state authorities and environmental protesters.
3 In Brandenburg, the charismatic SPD Minister President Manfred Stolpe was able to keep the SPD united and recover to win the subsequent Landtag electon of October 1994 with an absolute majority. In Bremen, where it was the SPD that split, the Greens increased their vote share, whilst the the SPD were

forced into a Grand Coalition with the CDU. Thus, the pattern appears to be that the electorate punishes intra-party strife.

4 Subsequent state elections in Mecklenburg-Vorpommern and Thuringen resulted in the failure of both the FDP and Greens to pass the 5 per cent electoral barrier.

4

'Then we take Berlin'

The relationship between the parties in West Berlin

From the late nineteenth century, Berlin has had a reputation as a centre for the political avant-garde. With the division of the city after the Second World War, the city assumed a special 'four-power' status that gave West Berlin what can only be described as a semi-detached place within the Federal Republic. Marooned over one hundred miles inside East Germany and exempt from the draft for military service that applied elsewhere in West Germany, the Western half of the divided city soon became a magnet for both politically active and alienated German youth. As a result, it was not surprising that the 'Berlin Alternative Liste' (AL) was one of the more radical local Green parties in the Federal Republic. Not only had it opposed the initial foundation of a Republic-wide Green party, but had maintained a semi-autonomous stance towards it. As Markovits and Gorski put it, the Berlin AL 'were in many respects closer in substance and spirit to the "Fundis" than the "Realos"' (1993: 231).

Because of this record of ideological fundamentalism, not only was co-operation with the CDU out of the question, but even co-operation with the SPD was the subject of intense internal discussion. Prior to the 1989 election, the AL portrayed such a strategy as being primarily a means of removing the incumbent CDU–FDP administration rather than as a positive move in itself. Yet even such a tentative stance towards the SPD was roundly condemned by many within the AL, highlighting the ideological and tactical struggle between the party's fundamentalist executive and relatively pragmatic parliamentary faction (*Der Tageszielung* (TAZ), 19 August 1988).

For its part, the Berlin SPD entered the election with a leader, Walter Momper, who represented the younger generation of SPD leaders personified by Oskar Lafontaine, Bjorn Engholm and Gerhard Schröder. The

1980s had not been a success for the Berlin SPD, who had lost two municipal elections in succession and were a long way from recovering their previously strong position in the city. Momper was not regarded as a strong enough candidate to defeat the CDU's charismatic Eberhard Diepgen, and opinion prior to the election foresaw another victory for the incumbent CDU–FDP coalition. Thus, prior to the 1989 elections, any possibility of the SPD regaining office lay in the possibility of a coalition agreement with the FDP, CDU or AL. As it turned out, the FDP was not to pass the Federal Republic's 5 per cent electoral barrier and the SPD's potential coalition partners consisted of just the CDU and AL.

The campaign, party programmes and bargaining

But how close, in policy terms, was the SPD to the other two parties? The Social Democrats were closer to the Greens on issues such as welfare policy, policing and individual freedom but had more in common with the CDU in both style and substance on the core issues of economic management and the city's position at the frontline of the cold war. Like the CDU, and unlike the AL, at no time did the SPD challenge the economic and political order that underpins modern industrial society. On the contrary, the SPD's instinct for more traditional corporatist solutions was demonstrated by its proposal for setting up an all-party commission to tackle Berlin's unemployment and environmental problems.

It is perhaps understandable that the Berlin SPD erred on the side of caution and the maintenance of the status quo. Prior to the fall of the Berlin Wall, the Four-Power Agreement endowed a peculiar constitutional status upon the city. Central to this status was the presence in West Berlin of the three Western Allies. The privileges that the Allies enjoyed as protecting powers was not only formally codified in West Berlin's constitution but, owing to the city's post-war experience, also possessed considerable normative power of its own. Because the Allied presence was so central to the city's identity and political discourse, attitudes towards it were arguably the litmus test of a party's wider political ideology. Thus, no self-consciously 'constitutional' party could seriously challenge the post-war settlement and, perhaps just as importantly, no truly 'anti-party party' could easily accommodate it. As a result, the differences on this issue within the two parties election literature are quite pronounced. The SPD supported the Allied presence (although it adopted a less bellicose attitude towards the Honecker regime than the CDU), whilst the AL

wanted it reduced to a 'symbolic remnant' (AL, 1990). Given this fundamental divide, it is not surprising that, following the elections, Momper
demanded clarification of the AL's stance towards this issue as proof of its
suitability as a coalition partner. The AL eventually did modify their
stance in order to enter government, which was a clear tactical victory for
Momper and the SPD.

There was, however, one distinct policy area that did provide opportunities for policy agreement between the SPD and the AL – internal security. Under the aegis of two successive CDU–FDP coalitions, and
originally in response to disorder related to the squatters' movement in
the early 1980s, the West Berlin police force expanded dramatically,
accompanied by the introduction of quite draconian operational tactics.[1]
These measures proved very popular with a significant proportion of the
population, to the extent that the CDU's 1989 manifesto pledged to continue this policing strategy: it stated that the police could 'count on the
support of the Berlin CDU' (CDU, 1989: 21). For the SPD, although
squatters and the like were not popular with their core voters, the issue
was contentious within the party's membership. Not only had the use of
the police become to some extent a partisan issue, but much of the left-
wing vote that they hoped to garner from the AL was highly critical of the
CDU's policy and had sympathy for the AL's stance, which refused to
draw any distinction between 'criminal' and 'state' violence. As a result
the AL demanded the abolition of the entire criminal code relating to
political violence (AL, 1990: 5–6). Although they did not go anything like
as far as the AL on the issue, the SPD did propose a policy of 'de-escalation' that moved its position much closer to the AL than to the CDU
(SPD, 1990: 22). Ironically, the policy of de-escalation was not only to
hamper the coalition from within weeks of its inception (when anarchist
'autonomous groups' began to open up new squats in an attempt to
embarrass the coalition), but would prove to be the issue that brought it
to a close.

Another area where the SPD and AL were close was with regard to what
could broadly be termed 'women's issues', although the SPD often sublimated this theme into other areas such as, for example, employment
rights and training. The SPD's proposals were, once again, less radical
than the AL's – who demanded a minimum quota of 50 per cent of all
work and training places for women – but still much more progressive
than the CDU's stance on the issue.[2] Moreover, Momper made it part of
his personal appeal to promote women into his putative Cabinet. Along
with the AL's clear commitment to the issue, the eventual representation

of women in the coalition would, at that time, be the highest ever in a state government, with women being given all three AL portfolios and six of the eleven SPD portfolios.

Another fruitful area of co-operation between the two parties was with regard to voting rights for foreigners. The CDU opposed the right of long-term foreign residents to vote in local elections, no doubt for reasons of electoral logic as well as a point of principle. But the SPD, the trade unions and the AL favoured such a right and proposed to lobby the Constitutional Court on the issue. This proposal was highly contested, but did provide a normatively powerful topic around which the coalition could mobilise.

One final example of an area where the SPD and AL were programmatically close was in the field of cultural politics, including the legacy of Germany's past. In a nation where symbols have such resonance, the debate over the nature of German culture is highly politicised. This was particularly true of the German Left, much of which is steeped in a belief in what Jurgen Habermas has called 'constitutional patriotism' (*Verfassungpatriotismus*), with its emphasis upon the existing reality of the Federal republic and its rejection of the older symbolism of the German nation (Markovits and Gorski, 1993: 276). In the context of Berlin, this debate was particularly fierce, not just because of the city's history but also because of the CDU–FDP administration's policies during the 1980s. The outgoing coalition invested a great deal of political as well as monetary capital in a number of prestige projects, designed to re-establish Berlin's reputation as a 'world city'. The most controversial of these was the planned German Historical Museum, which both the AL and SPD rejected as inappropriate and proposed to scrap. Both parties rejected the previous concentration upon centralised, capital-intensive projects and planned to introduce a more decentralised and heterogeneous policy, which they regarded as more in keeping with the multi-cultural reality of late 1980s Berlin.

In short, a comparison of party programmes indicates that the SPD was the only party able to find common ideological ground with both the other parties in the new West Berlin parliament. If it chose, it could profile the more socially conservative and authoritarian side of its ideological profile in order to bargain with the CDU, or it could pursue a more post-materialist, New Left-oriented agenda in order to bargain with the AL. Prior to the elections, the SPD was in a potentially strong position. As it turned out, their share of the vote virtually ensured their place in government.

The results of the city elections of 29 January 1989 were greeted with mixed feelings by West Berlin's political class. The SPD won a slim victory, with 41.7 per cent of the first vote and 37.3 per cent of the second vote. This gave them 55 out of 138 seats in the new parliament. The CDU gained the same number of seats, on the basis of slightly less first votes (40.2 per cent) but more second votes (37.7 per cent). The Greens scored 11.1 per cent and 11.8 per cent respectively, giving them seventeen seats, whilst the FDP's vote share fell below the 5 per cent needed to enter parliament. But the euphoria surrounding the possibility of a change of government was dampened by the success of the far-right Republican party, who gained 7.5 per cent of second votes and eleven seats in the new parliament.

The failure of the FDP meant that the CDU had to look elsewhere for coalition partners if it was to muster the seventy seats needed for a legislative majority. But their room for manoeuvre was constrained by the presence of the Republican party. The legacy of Germany's past has continued to put such parties beyond the pale as potential coalition partners. But the CDU also ruled out any bargaining with the AL and even tried to equate them with the Republicans (*TAZ*, 10 February 1989). This was clearly an attempt to limit the SPD's options to the CDU's advantage. To this end, Diepgen adopted a high media profile: he gave numerous interviews in which he stressed what he saw as the potential danger to West Berlin of a Red–Green coalition, and asserted the CDU's claim to be the strongest political force in the city. Diepgen made it clear what he expected from the SPD, describing any future SPD–AL coalition as 'not very tenable' and the possibility of a CDU-tolerated SPD minority government as 'not very plausible'. Diepgen re-emphasised what he described as the CDU's 'claim to leadership' of the Berlin government (*TAZ*, 2 February 1989).

Despite Diepgen's efforts, it was apparent at the time that the real initiative lay with the SPD. In electoral terms, the SPD had made substantial gains over the previous election (up 9.3 per cent) and had fulfilled Momper's declared aim of breaking the CDU–FDP hegemony in Berlin (*TAZ*, 22 October 1988). The high degree of ideological polarisation in the new legislature, and the SPD's ideological location in the centre of it, virtually assured it of a place in government. But this polarisation also meant that the SPD would have to exercise political skill if it was to exploit its position to the full without alienating either of its two prospective coalition partners. In this, the Berlin SPD were lucky enough to have been led by Momper, even though prior to the election he had not been particularly highly regarded. Coming from the 'New Left' tendency within the SPD, Momper had a history of support and involvement in left-wing causes, including protest activity against the Allied presence in West Berlin (Mattox and Bradley Shingleton (eds), 1992: 68). In this sense he came from the same milieu as many in the AL. At the same time, however, he was a pragmatic politician and had moderated both his policy stance and political style since assuming the SPD leadership. Thus, whilst asserting that the result of the election signalled a desire on the part of the electorate for a 'new, social, liberal and ecological reform-politics' (*TAZ*, 1 February 1989), Momper also stressed that he intended to enter into negotiations with both the AL and CDU with no prior preferences (*TAZ*, 2 February 1989). So skilful was Momper's performance during this period of coalition bargaining that an editorial in the *TAZ*, written after the formal codification of the SPD–AL coalition, described it as that of a 'skilful, unscrupulous and power-conscious tactician' (*TAZ*, 18 February 1989). It could be argued that Momper's task was made easier by tactical naiveté on the part of the AL. Not only had the AL made the removal of the incumbent CDU–FDP administration its primary electoral goal, but its spokesperson had even speculated in public about the AL tolerating an SPD minority government for an interim period. This could hardly be described as keeping one's powder dry!

One can speculate as to why one of the more fundamentalist Green parties in the Federal Republic chose to embark on such a strategy and they might have been aware that where similar tactical dilemmas had arisen elsewhere in Germany, a strategy of non-co-operation or even confrontation with the SPD had proven counter-productive (Markovits and Gorski, 1993: 202). But this evidence is not conclusive, as other local variables, such as local political personalities, have to be taken into account. Although Momper had expressed no interest in new elections, the possibility remained that they might have been called in the event of an impasse. Therefore, it is possible that the AL calculated that a strategy of not co-operating with the SPD could place them in a no-win situation, resulting in either a Grand Coalition between the CDU and SPD or new elections, after which the AL's bargaining position could be come considerably worse. Beyond such bargaining logic, there was considerable pressure from the grass roots to negotiate with the SPD on the grounds of policy. There were some policy domains within which there were real possibilities for agreement. On the other hand, there were areas where the two parties held potentially incompatible positions. Moreover the AL was, arguably, disadvantaged in as much as the SPD could claim a wider mandate, not just numerically but as a 'catch-all' party. As a *TAZ* article ruefully observed, 'the SPD bargained – even if true or not – in the name of the Berliners and in the name of a politicised, mistrustful city, the AL bargained only in the name of its grass-roots' (*TAZ*, 7 March 1989). Given the residual normative and numerical weight of the SPD, the AL was, perhaps inevitably, at a disadvantage during the bargaining process.

After two rounds of negotiations in the first weeks of February, it had become clear that the SPD was not prepared to recognise the CDU's 'claim to leadership'. But there were still barriers to co-operation with the AL. In the context of a deteriorating situation in the city's finances, and what almost amounted to panic amongst some elements of the business community at the thought of the AL in government, Momper engaged in widespread consultations with trade unions, employers' organisations and other civic groups, during which he spelt out his plans for tackling unemployment and the skills deficit in the city. Despite these difficulties, Momper was clearly gaining the upper hand in the bargaining process.

One might have expected the AL to be enjoying its pivotal role with regard to the two big parties. But in reality the AL's options were limited, and provoked considerable bitterness towards the SPD, as well as the inevitable internal disagreement. Clearly, any form of co-operation with an establishment party will present both ideological and tactical difficulties for Green parties. For the Berlin AL these were focused on the fact that the SPD was competing with them by co-opting some elements of 'their' post-materialist agenda.

The process of coalition negotiation following the January elections took a number of weeks. Although the rank and file of both parties were overwhelmingly in favour of such a coalition, the AL's 'fundi' wing were not in favour of parliamentary co-operation, whilst there remained some elements within the local SPD elite who regarded the AL as a radical left-wing party and not a suitable coalition partner (Jun, 1994: 218). Indeed it has been suggested that local SPD leader Walter Momper was privately less than enthusiastic for such a coalition.

Most public disagreement occurred over the division of Cabinet posts between the parties. This manifested itself in a long, acrimonious and very public process of bargaining. Six weeks after the election, an AL spokesperson stated that the party still awaited an acceptable offer from the SPD and criticised the SPD's 'unfair bargaining style' (*TAZ*, 10 March 1989). The crucial issue that divided the two parties was the form and allocation of the portfolio for women's issues. The AL demanded that this portfolio should be a Ministerial post in its own right and, naturally, that it should be allocated to them. Eventually, a compromise was reached. On the 13 March, the SPD and AL agreed the composition of the city government. The AL did indeed receive the women's issues brief, albeit sublimated within a wider Ministry.

In purely numerical terms, the AL did not do as well as the SPD in terms of the division of portfolios. The 29 January elections had resulted in the election to the city legislature of seventeen AL representatives and fifty-five from the SPD. But the AL received only three out of the fourteen Cabinet posts on offer: a ratio of legislative seats to Cabinet posts of almost six-to-one. By contrast, the SPD ratio was just five-to-one, in addition to which Walter Momper became Governing Mayor. At first glance, this would seem peculiar given that the AL arguably held the balance of power, and could be interpreted as another indication of political naiveté on their part. Yet such a narrow interpretation ignores the fact that certain policy sectors, such as the environment, held disproportionate weight for the AL. Moreover, the coupling of city development and traffic policy with environmental protection (rather than with construction and housing, for example) was considered a hard fought and essential victory for the AL in the teeth of SPD opposition. As one member of the former AL city-parliament grouping observed 'we didn't want just a Ministry for environmental propaganda. We wanted to make policy' (Interview).

Internal and external constraints, staffing and expertise

When the West Berlin Red–Green coalition came to power in 1989, it was clear that, by any objective criteria, the city was confronted by a backlog of serious economic and environmental problems. These stemmed from both the peculiar geographical position of Berlin as well as its internal economy and structure. Since the beginning of the cold war, the city's links with its immediate surroundings had been constrained by the Berlin Wall. This meant that everything from transport and energy provision to waste disposal and pollution control had developed in a somewhat fractured and *ad-hoc* basis, in response to the problems of maintaining a capitalist enclave over 100 miles inside the Eastern bloc. The city was dependent upon the co-operation of the German Democratic Republic yet unintegrated with it (for obvious reasons), whilst politically tied to the Federal Republic, yet geographically distant. The city was subject to (indeed, its own status often aggravated) the prevailing state of inter-German relations, so that such agreements that existed were primarily concerned with trade and travel and operated within quite rigid parameters. The German Democratic Republic's own environmental record was appalling and the effects of this, particularly its debilitating reliance upon brown coal, were directly felt in West Berlin in the form of its own forced over-reliance upon brown coal, and severe particulate air pollution (manifesting itself in frequent smog alarms during the winter months). These external constraints contributed to the relative economic weakness of the West Berlin economy and the often poor state of its own environment. The obvious need to ecologically modernise the economy was not only recognised by the AL but also by the mainstream parties. Thus, although the SPD was still constrained by the traditional materialist discourse and saw the maintenance of jobs as equally important, there was some commonality with the Greens about the problems the city faced.

With regard to specific problem areas, both parties identified in their election literature the most pressing areas of environmental concern as those of waste disposal, housing, transport and energy policy. But, as would be expected, the AL's proposals were more radical and less concerned with their impact upon economic growth and employment. Indeed, their election literature carried an implicit rejection of growth as a primary economic objective. Their proposals were embedded in what can be described as a 'non-administrative' discourse that was almost evangelical in style but lacked policy detail.[3] This polemical style contrasted with the more measured and specific proposals put forward by the SPD (SPD Ländesverband Berlin, 1988: 9).

Nevertheless, three points have to be considered when making this comparison, which apply to the Niedersachsen case as well. First, as the Greens in Germany are not a 'deep green' party but rather a left-libertarian/'New Politics' party (albeit with a strong ecological component within their ideological profile), environmental policy was not dealt with as a discreet self-standing policy area but rather embedded within a more far-reaching discourse about the nature of power within society. Second, given that the AL contained such disparate elements, the local party was more effective when playing a 'mobilising' role for the broad green agenda than when dealing with specifics. This was not only because gaining office was less of an immediate priority, but also because conflicts between the competing strands of party thought soon became apparent when dealing with these specifics. In other words, the party agreed more about what it was against than the detailed nature of the society it was actually working towards (Scharf, 1994, Hülsberg, 1988, Markovits and Gorski, 1993, etc.). Finally, given the Greens' 'outsider' status and their relatively non-hierarchical structure, they lacked the policy-making resources of the established parties and had to rely upon outside expertise (see Poguntke, 1989 for instance). Thus, policy-formulation processes did exist, but in a more decentralised and less visible fashion than within the SPD. In the West Berlin case, the AL were able to harness the rich pool of environmental expertise centred around the city's universities (in particular the Free University). If one was to use Rhodes' (1986a) typology of policy networks to describe these resources, the Greens only had access to an 'issue network' (characterised by a number of participants, a limited degree of interdependence and a relatively atomised structure), albeit a reasonably well-established one.

The coalition took office to a mixed reception from West Berlin's intermediary organisations. Opposition from employers' organisations – as in Hessen – took the form of dire warnings of 'Red–Green chaos' and a further deterioration in the city's economic circumstances. Still it is interesting to note that the outcry from employers lacked the vitriolic edge that greeted the appointment of Joschka Fischer as Environment Minister in Hessen. One reason why this was so in West Berlin was because Langmann's threats had rapidly been exposed as essentially empty and ineffective (Grant, Paterson and Whitston, 1988: 253), and was perhaps also an early indicator that the Greens were becoming marginally less stigmatised within the German polity. Essentially, the employers took a 'wait and see' attitude, possibly reflecting the widespread belief, articulated by CDU leader Diepgen, that the coalition would soon collapse under its own internal contradictions (*TAZ*, 2 February 1989).

Equally predictably – but from the SPD's point of view more worrying – was the reaction of the local trade unions to the new coalition. The traditionally right-wing unions, such as the construction workers' union (IG BSE), displayed outright hostility to the idea of a Red–Green coalition, but the education and science union (GEW), which had quite strong links with the AL (Schools' Minister Sybille Volkholz had been a union official) was far more sympathetic to the idea. There was a marked correlation between the stance of individual unions, the producer interests they represented and the priority given to certain areas of policy by the new coalition, with the coalition committed to an early expansion of nursery education and crèche facilities, but displaying a more ambiguous attitude towards the building sector.

Amongst the permanent civil service, attitudes towards the new coalition were also mixed. The established political parties staffed a high proportion of civil service posts and, given the eight-year incumbency of the previous administration, it was to be assumed that a significant proportion of civil servants were CDU or FDP members. This trend was particularly pronounced amongst the top tier of permanent officials, who were often political appointees. Under German law these officials enjoyed security of tenure and could not be sacked, although they could be granted indefinite leave at the public expense. Whilst it could be expected that some, especially the more senior and/or well-connected officials, would retire or move on, incoming Ministers wanting to make major changes were confronted with the cost of keeping superfluous civil servants on the payroll and finding men and women of sufficient credibility and expertise to replace them. Traditionally, this would not have been a problem given the degree of consensus inherent in the German policy community but there were fears that, with the entry of the AL into government, this consensus would break down. Thus there was a danger that the new coalition could be hampered by what could best be described as 'implementation drag' on the part of recalcitrant officials. Indeed, internal resistance within the Schools, Training and Sport Ministry reached such a degree that, as one SPD official put it, 'sabotage was mentioned' (Interview).

This implementation drag does not appear to have taken place within the Greens' key portfolio, the City Development, Environmental Protection and Traffic Ministry. There appear to be three reasons for this. First, as the Ministry was only set up in 1981, it had not been 'captured' or become part of a rigid policy network (based on producer interests) in the manner of some of the more established Ministries. Second, it was staffed with younger officials who appeared to be relatively well-disposed to the idea of ecological modernisation policies and therefore more open to innovation. Third, the Ministry had previously been close to the FDP and – as they had failed to pass West Berlin's 5 per cent electoral barrier – they were not represented in the legislature. Thus, any latent opposition that did exist amongst permanent officials lacked a parliamentary focus. As a result, the new Environment Minister and her staff were confident that they could successfully implement the agreed programme.

The programme placed emphasis upon greater transparency in what they called the city's 'planning culture'. Other specific commitments included new controls over air emissions and the encouragement of new clean air technologies, removal of lead piping and the imposition of state-of-the-art technology within the water industry, improved river management, imposition of an integrated and coherent waste disposal policy in co-operation with other German states, a freeze on the new development of green field sites, the development and imposition of what was trumpeted as a 'rational and socially sustainable' system of energy provision and use (including a new energy tax), the modification of existing laws on energy use, a long-term plan to completely re-open the city's railway system (S-Bahn), the expansion of public transport through extension of bus-lanes, reduced waiting times, and, finally, the reduction of fares including the introduction of a cheap all-inclusive travel pass called the 'environment card' (*Umweltkarte*).

Three main observations can be made about the coalition's proposed programme. First, with the exception of some aspects of transport policy (for instance, the reduction of fares for public transport, introduction of the 'environment card' and the imposition of traffic controls) most of the programme required implementation over the medium to long term. This meant that political costs (such as funding that would have otherwise gone on construction and service provision) were felt immediately, whilst the benefits were either deferred or intangible. Second, as noted above, the policy document was the product of two distinct and often contradictory discourses. The left-libertarian/post-materialist-oriented linkage between environmental policy and wider societal power structures is plainly evident in, for instance, the greater role allocated to local communities in future planning decisions, and the opening out of the policy community through horizontally structured 'working groups' and the inclusion of non-governmental organisations, etc. At the same time, a more statist approach remains evident and arguably could hardly have been avoided, given that the coalition remained reliant upon the existing civil service to, for instance, recodify law, administer increased subsidies to public transport and collect eco-taxes. This tension between the two approaches is evident in much of the policy documentation produced over the life of the West Berlin coalition. Finally, there was a primary reliance upon bureaucratic instruments (such as judicial review, state regulation and subsidy), with economic instruments (such as eco-taxes and pricing) taking a secondary role. This was especially so in dealing with indivisible public goods, such as air and water, and is in keeping with traditions of public policy in the Federal Republic. This reliance upon bureaucratic instruments represented continuity rather than change in the coalition's style of policy making (Lees, 1998).

The politics and policies of the Berlin coalition

The coalition agreement between the SPD and AL was formally codified on 13 March 1989. Three days later, the appointment of West Berlin's new executive was ratified by the city's legislature amid a mood of some optimism. As an article in the *TAZ* remarked at the time, the ratification process had passed with an ease that was unprecedented in the recent history of West Berlin's relatively polarised local politics. As to why this was the case, the *TAZ* – despite its often critical attitude towards the Berlin SPD – gave most of the credit to the negotiating skills of the SPD's Walter Momper (*TAZ*, 18 March 1989).

For Momper, this was the high point of his career. Written off by many commentators before the election as a political lightweight, the subsequent bargaining process revealed another side to his character. In doing so, he had established the primacy of the SPD in the coalition, with the AL apparently content to take the role of junior partner. After the vote of ratification, Governing Mayor Momper walked to the podium and prophesised that 'the great unity shown by both governing factions in today's vote is also a sign and signal of the predictability and stability of this coalition' (Abgeordnetenhaus von Berlin, *Plenarprotokollen*, Band i. 1 bis 18. Sitzung, 1991: 37).

At the time, such optimism did not seem misplaced. The coalition had a reasonable gender balance and had drawn up a progressive reform programme. With Federal elections due in 1990, and Helmut Kohl and the CDU/CSU–FDP coalition doing badly in the polls, there was some degree of speculation amongst SPD and AL activists at least that successful co-operation between their parties could even provide a model for government in Bonn (*TAZ*, 15 February 1989). Yet by the time those elections took place, the Berlin Wall had fallen, Germany was unified, a triumphant Kohl returned to the Chancellery in Bonn and the Berlin coalition had collapsed in disarray and mutual recrimination. The AL, who had left the coalition and tabled a vote of no confidence in Momper, were accused by him of irresponsibility and pursuing a perverse form of 'scorched earth' politics (*TAZ*, 17 November 1990). In reply, the AL's Christian Strobele declared that the real problem lay with the SPD's cautious approach to the reform agenda. But Strobele also observed that policy disagreements 'were not always the SPD's fault, as they must consider completely different sections of the electorate than we would want to and have to' (*TAZ*, 17 November 1990).

So what went wrong? The German political sociologist Gudrun Heinrich has described the Berlin Red–Green coalition as having three distinct phases. The first phase, lasting from the Spring until late Summer of 1989, can be described as the coalition's 'honeymoon period'. The second phase, lasting from the late Summer of 1989 until early 1990, was characterised by a slow breakdown in trust between the two parties. The third and final phase, lasting from the beginning of 1990 until its collapse was, in Heinrich's words, characterised by 'two parties governing next to and against each other, with no joint strategy to follow' (1993: 39). Obviously the cataclysmic changes of November 1989 completely transformed the political environment within which the coalition was trying to function and must have put an enormous strain upon the participants. The breakdown in relations between the two parties was striking, and played out in the full view of the wider German polity.

As soon as the coalition was inaugurated, it was put under pressure. Elements from the 'autonomous groups' (who enjoyed links with elements of the AL arising out of the Berlin squatters' movement of the early 1980s) promptly squatted a number of flats in the Kreuzberg area of the city. This was widely regarded as an explicit act of provocation of a coalition of which the autonomous groups disapproved wholeheartedly. The squatting action presented the AL with a conflict between the priorities of party management and coalition maintenance. Given that the AL had entered into the coalition against the wishes of elements of its own milieu, it was loath to further antagonise them by moving against the squatters. On the other hand, the SPD Interior Minister Erich Pätzold was determined to hold the line against such an early challenge to his own authority and, by definition, that of the coalition. As a result, Pätzold demanded and obtained the reluctant support of his AL colleagues in clearing the squatters (*TAZ*, 23 March 1989).

This first skirmish with the squatters' groups highlighted a fundamental tension within the coalition. Like any political party, the AL needed to deliver tangible results for its client groups in order to maintain party unity. At the same time, it needed to give its parliamentary elite a free hand, both in its dealings with the SPD and as a party of government in its own right. But inevitably some elements of the AL's milieu had interests antithetical to the AL's status as a coalition partner. Although the Red–Green coalition enjoyed the support of the majority of the AL's members and voters, the AL's internal structure – or lack of it – allowed vociferous minorities to make their views heard. The AL's system of delegational democracy meant that members of its parliamentary faction (including coalition Ministers) were required to regularly report back to the party caucus. These caucus meetings were often quite heated and, now that the AL was in government, very well-reported. As a result Berliners were now treated to the spectacle of AL Ministers being cross examined by their local caucus on the evening news. Inevitably, there was no shortage of highly quotable members of the 'counter-culture', ready to play to the prejudices of ordinary Berliners. It all looked frighteningly like the much-promised 'Red–Green chaos'!

For the AL Ministers themselves, and for much of their rank and file, it was soon apparent that the responsibilities of government could be quite uncomfortable. As Heinrich observes, the early days of the coalition demonstrated to the AL that they now 'had to go along with decisions that they had previously opposed' (1993: 42). The first few months of government saw the AL in the thick of the action and forced into making contentious decisions. The first big row within the coalition concerned the planned extension of the city's prestigious Rudolf Virchow Clinic, under plans agreed by the previous CDU–FDP administration. The AL opposed the project, on the grounds that it went against the principle of decentralisation and the enhancement of mobile community-based care facilities. But in June 1989, the AL Ministers eventually gave in and approved the extension plans on the grounds that they were so far under-way and alternative plans did not exist. In addition, the two coalition parties fell out over a planned border crossing to the GDR. Although an elite compromise was eventually reached, the AL's Plenary Session[4] rejected this and called on its representatives in the legislature to do all they could to stop the border crossing coming about (Heinrich, 1993: 41).

In addition to these internal disagreements, the coalition found itself up against the powerful motorists' lobby, following a decision to impose a 100 kilometres per hour speed limit on West Berlin's only stretch of motorway, the AVUS. Although justifiable on environmental grounds, the AVUS decision was bad politics. Overnight, the motorists' association ADAC was gifted with an issue around which to mobilise opposition to the coalition.

Both parties seemed aware of the significance of their political co-operation. This was clearly demonstrated by a number of press conferences held in June 1989 to celebrate and take stock of the first hundred days of the coalition. For its part, the AL deemed the first phase of the coalition a success, although they felt that the realities of government had eroded any initial euphoria. They now regarded the coalition as a 'high risk and exciting experiment' in government (AL Pressestelle, 26 June 1989). For its part, the SPD was satisfied with the first 100 days, but were beginning to show signs of frustration and impatience at the slow pace of decision-making within the coalition. The blame for this was put squarely at the AL's door, because of their insistence on referring everything back to their local caucus. As Momper observed, the AL had to 'develop (internal) structures that would make the entire coalition more capable of taking decisions' (Press Statement by Momper, 23 June 1989). The first phase of the coalition was coming to an end.

No sooner had the one hundred-day honeymoon period been passed than the coalition entered its first really major crisis. The cause of the crisis was an agreement between the local city-owned electricity generator BEWAG and Preussen Electra and Intrac to supply electricity between the GDR and Berlin. The contract had been closed by the previous CDU–FDP administration, but was vehemently opposed by the AL. As a result, the coalition agreement stated that the coalition intended to 'cancel or make adjustments' to the contract once in power (SPD Berlin, 1989: 23). For many in the AL, this issue was a fundamental test of the coalition's environmental credentials (Heinrich, 1993: 42). Unfortunately for the AL, the policy area fell within the remit of SPD Economics Minister Peter Mitzscherling, who proposed that the contract should go ahead. Mitzscherling's decision was vehemently opposed by the AL's Michaele Schreyer, whose Ministry for City Development and Environmental Protection also had competencies in this field. The AL Ministry also had access to advice from a circle of environmental initiative groups, research centres and individual activists, who also opposed the plan. As a result of this overlap of powers, both the Economics Ministry and the Ministry for City Development and Environmental Protection undertook a review of the legal basis of the contract.

On the 22 September 1989, a special plenum of the AL passed a resolution stating their implacable opposition to the contract going ahead. The plenum issued an imperative mandate to the AL parliamentary faction, making the issue the benchmark of continued co-operation with the SPD. Implicit in the AL's critique was what they called their 'dissatisfaction with the timid implementation of certain elements of the coalition agreement' (Protocol of the AL Plenary session of 22 September 1989, cited Heinrich, 1993: 43). The final decision on the contract was an exercise in political brinkmanship. But the SPD made it clear that any veto of the contract would signal the end of the coalition and, in December 1989, the AL Ministers reluctantly gave their consent to the agreement.

The next major source of conflict within the coalition began in late November and early December of 1989, with the onset of strike action by care workers at children's day-care centres, known as KITAS, with the aim of improving pay and working conditions, and in particular the achievement of an agreement on a minimum wage. The AL, who enjoyed substantial support amongst KITA workers, came out clearly in favour of the demands of the strikers. But Interior Minister Pätzold rejected the strikers' demands, with the support of the rest of the SPD. Again, the AL had found itself in the ambiguous situation of both being in power and advocating a stance that was implicitly in opposition to the stance adopted by the coalition as a whole. After ten weeks the strike collapsed without success.

At this point the AL were in an invidious situation. On several occasions they had found themselves in a situation where they were unable to defend the interests of their client groups against the decisions of the city government as a whole. This prompted the AL's extra-parliamentary organisation to issue a harsh critique of the actions of the coalition and demand, despite the fact that the strike had failed, that negotiations on the subject of the minimum wage should start immediately. The AL's demands fell on deaf ears and, at the plenum of 24 March 1990, Heidi Bischoff-Pflanz (the chair of the AL's parliamentary faction and a vociferous supporter of the KITA strike) announced her resignation. Frau Bischoff-Pflanz was widely regarded as a representative of the AL's left wing. This meant that her support had been essential in maintaining intra-party peace and support for the coalition. The Red–Green coalition was entering its final phase.

The last phase of the West Berlin Red–Green coalition coincided with the final stages of the process of German unification. Therefore it is perhaps fitting that one of the major sources of conflict between the parties in these final months concerned the sale of 61,710 square metres of real estate on the Potsdamer Platz to the Daimler-Benz concern. The initial negotiations between Governing Mayor Momper, Minister for Construction and Housing Wolfgang Nagel and Daimler-Benz had taken place in the summer of 1989. As Heinrich observes, the intervening months had transformed the Potsdamer Platz from waste ground on the edge of the Allied-occupied city to the centre of a re-united Berlin (Heinrich, 1993: 47). But by the time that the AL and, indeed, the SPD as a whole were informed, the deal had gone through. This not only aggravated the already sensitive feelings of the AL, but also significant elements of the SPD itself. At issue was not only the fact that the changed circumstances of the area had rendered the sale price ridiculously low, but also that the sale of what was now prime real estate raised questions as to the suitabil-

ity of the Daimler Benz building being sited in the centre of a new unified
Berlin. The fact that the deal was going ahead, combined with the manner in which it had been arranged and announced, made a mockery of the
idea of integrated and environmentally sound city planning.

Such a plan was within the remit of the Ministry for City Development
and Environmental Protection, whose Minister Michaele Schreyer was
now on the verge of resignation. By the time that the contract with Daimler Benz was signed in June 1990, relations between the two coalition
partners had reached a new low. The deal went ahead on the strength of
the votes of the SPD and CDU in the legislature, with the AL voting
against. In effect, this meant that the SPD had implicitly sidelined Frau
Schreyer and undermined the principle of Ministerial autonomy. The
Daimler Benz debacle led the AL to debate their continued participation
in the coalition. The debate, which took place on the 15 and 16 June 1990,
was given added urgency because, following the first free elections of 6
May 1990, East Berlin was now governed by a Grand Coalition between
the SPD and CDU. At this point, Momper announced proposals to send
West Berlin Ministers over to East Berlin in order to take over responsibilities as a precursor to unification of the two city governments (Heinrich, 1993: 48). The initiative failed in the teeth of the opposition of both
the AL and SPD activists, but it was clear that the rules of the game had
changed and the AL had got the message.

By the early autumn of 1990, the AL's grass roots membership was in
almost open defiance of the coalition and the mood amongst activists was
now openly in favour of ending political co-operation with the SPD. This
process precipitated a major crisis of party management for the AL when,
in August 1990, fifty-one leading left wingers declared that they were now
'going into opposition to the majority of the AL' (Heinrich, 1993: 49).
The rebels even suggested that the AL was in danger of self-destructing
over the issue. Clearly, if the AL was going to hold together as a party, it
had to find an issue around which it could mobilise.

The next source of conflict between the SPD and the AL concerned the
future of a Research Reactor at the city's Hahn-Meitner Research Institute
(HMI). Like the contract between the electricity generators, the AL
regarded the cancellation of the reactor project as a test of the coalition's
environmental credentials and, again, the SPD appeared to be back slid-
ing on the issue. As a result the AL Minister for City Development and
Environmental Protection Schreyer found herself in direct conflict with
the SPD Minister for Science and Research, Barbara Riedmuller-Seel. In
May 1990, despite the overlap in competencies between her Ministry and

that of Schreyer, Riedmuller-Seel had unilaterally given the go-ahead to the reactor coming on-line, although the final decision was put back until August. At the beginning of August, at the behest of the SPD, the legislature ordered Schreyer to confirm Riedmuller-Seel's decision within two weeks (*Süddeutsche Zeitung*, 9 August 1990). Citing technical advice, Schreyer refused to comply and resigned.

Clearly, the coalition was falling apart, and only needed a sufficiently emotive issue to kill it off. Indeed, with new all-Berlin elections just around the corner, it could be argued that it suited both parties to do just that, in order to profile themselves to their supporters and mobilise their full electoral potential (Jun, 1994: 219). The Berlin Red–Green coalition's first big test, in the early days of government, involved the squatters' movement. It was apt, therefore, that it was another squatters' action that precipitated the final collapse of the coalition. On 15 November, SPD Interior Minister Pätzold ordered the eviction of a number of squatted houses in East Berlin's Mainzer Straße. In the aftermath of the evictions, there were serious street disturbances in the city. The AL responded with a press statement in which they declared that they 'were no longer prepared …to share responsibility for these policies' (Heinrich, 1993: 51). The Berlin Red–Green coalition was at an end.

Notes

1 One notorious example of such tactics occurred during the World Bank/International Monetary Fund (IMF) conference in 1987. Fearing protest demonstrations marching on the venue, the city government ordered the complete sealing-off of the city's Kreuzberg district. During this time, no-one was allowed in or out of the entire SO36 postal district.

2 The SPD proposed to expand the provision of nursery education by 10,000 places in four years. They also proposed a night-taxi service for women (which was eventually implemented). The CDU proposed some limited measures, but made it clear that these were to help women better manage their responsibilities at work and at home! (CDU, 1989: 10).

3 For instance, in the AL's main election pamphlet, the party's ecological proposals are summed up within a few lines of polemic: 'Ecology must take precedence over short-term economic interests. We need less consumption of raw materials and energy, [more] decontamination, less refuse, less traffic, less noise, less concrete and therefore more public transport, more ecological raw materials, more green, more free-time, more responsibility and more democracy … money should be spent on proposals that are made with regard to ecological and social criteria' (Alternative Liste Berlin, 1989: 3).

4   The Plenary Session, or Mitgliedsvollversammlung (MVV), was – in the tra-
    dition of delegational democracy – the highest decision-making body within
    the AL.

5

Niedersachsen and the irresistible rise of Gerhard Schröder

The relationship between the parties in Niedersachsen

By the late 1980s, the Niedersachsen polity was entering the final phase of the so-called 'Albrecht era', which lasted from 1978 until 1990. These years were characterised by a period of CDU hegemony in which, either alone or with the FDP as junior partner, the Christian Democrats, led by Ernst Albrecht, had run the state and excluded the SPD from power. By 1989, however, the CDU–FDP administration was looking a little ragged round the edges. Opinion polls showed a rise in support for the political extremes, as well as a growth in support for the idea of a Red–Green coalition along the lines of the Berlin coalition that had come to power earlier that year.

Niedersachsen was far more rural and conservative than West Berlin and this was reflected in the relatively conservative value orientation of the local SPD, which had been far more suspicious of the Greens than their Berlin counterparts. It was significant that the Niedersachsen SPD refused to rule out the possibility of a coalition with the Greens following the 1990 state elections *Die Frankfurter Allgemeine Zeitung (FAZ)*, 25 February 1989. For their part, the Niedersachsen Greens had explicitly campaigned for the removal of the Albrecht administration and its replacement with a Red–Green alternative. This was to seriously hinder their room for manoeuvre after the elections (*Neue Presse*, 18 May 1990).

Despite the obvious differences between the two states, the parallel with Berlin stuck in the public mind and the press began to speculate as to whether Albrecht could succeed where Eberhard Diepgen had failed and remain in power. The opinion polls at this time showed the CDU vote dropping, whilst the FDP's support appeared to be around 12 per cent (albeit on the strength of second votes from CDU supporters). If the CDU–FDP administration was to continue in power, it had to make a success of a raft of FDP-inspired fiscal reforms. However, perhaps as a result of the debilitating effects of a long period in office or because of the tense pre-election atmosphere, these reforms were becoming increasingly contentious within the coalition itself. As a result, Albrecht and his parliamentary faction leader Gansäuer came under fire for making too many concessions to the FDP. Many CDU colleagues argued that, in the run-up to the state elections, the FDP would need to profile themselves against their coalition partners whatever concessions were made.

For its part, the SPD kept up the pressure on the coalition. The SPD's parliamentary faction leader Gerhard Schröder had introduced what had been described as 'a new sharpness' into political debate (*Hannoversche Allgemeine Zeitung* (*HAZ*), 24 April 1990) and the party harried the coalition across a range of issues. By the December of 1988, they had unsuccessfully brought a motion of no-confidence in the coalition's financial management and, in particular, Albrecht's role in the Federal tax reforms (which came into operation in 1989). Albrecht was politically exposed on the issue because, as a member of the national CDU Presidium, he had been involved in the approval of the reforms, even though Niedersachsen had suffered a revenue loss of DM 1.2 billion as a result. Albrecht had managed to partially offset this loss by securing DM 680 million of structural funds from the Federal government, but he remained exposed on this issue (*FAZ*, 25 February 1989). The SPD responded by campaigning with the slogan 'down with the tax reforms' and proposed an additional means of aiding the regions. The SPD proposed a plan whereby 50 per cent of social security payments from the Federation to local government would be held back and used as direct aid to the most disadvantaged local communities. This tactic was a classic example of Schröder at his most unashamedly populist. The plan had, prior to the Federal tax reforms, been known as the 'Albrecht Plan', because it had originally been a product of the CDU-run State Chancellory. With Albrecht compromised by his federal role, Schröder was free to plunder the CDU's own policies and use them against the coalition.

As the state elections approached, the CDU and FDP put their differences aside and called a press conference where they praised each other's 'good work under difficult conditions' across the economic, social, ecological and cultural fields. Albrecht stated that, bearing in mind that it had only enjoyed a majority of one, the CDU–FDP coalition had been 'the best functioning coalition' in the Federal Republic (*HAZ*, 25 April 1990). The chances of its continuation looked favourable as well. CDU faction-chief Gansäuer pointed to an opinion poll in the run-up to the election that gave the CDU 43.5 per cent, the SPD 42.5 per cent, with both the FDP and the Greens on 6.5 per cent of the vote. The poll also indicated that 55 per cent of voters expected a CDU–FDP victory on 13 May. Moreover, Schröder lagged badly behind Albrecht as the popular choice for Minister President,[1] whilst 59 per cent of those polled thought that a Red–Green coalition would be bad for Niedersachsen. As the parties went into the state elections, there was little to indicate that a there would be any change in the governing coalition at the state parliament.

The campaign, party programmes and bargaining

By the end of the Albrecht era, the party system in Niedersachsen had polarised into two competing blocs. One bloc consisted of the outgoing government coalition of the CDU and FDP, who were opposed by a de facto Red–Green bloc of the SPD and Greens. According to Jun, this process of polarisation first became evident in the early 1970s. Whilst neither of the two big parties were able decisively to dominate the party system, the CDU was able to win a majority of the seats in 1978 and 1982 by taking advantage of the SPD's problems at the Federal level. But in 1986 the CDU could only remain in power with the help of the FDP. Thus, although the CDU and FDP were ostensibly in some form of electoral competition with one another, they were equally fighting on their joint record in government. Jun argues that the rise of the Greens, and the inability of the SPD to unseat the coalition, had aggravated this process. As a result, voters were in no doubt that they were voting for either a continuation of the existing administration or a Red–Green coalition (1994: 192–3). The perception of the voters was reinforced by the pronouncements of the politicians themselves. Although the SPD had made a point of keeping its coalition options open, Schröder was not popular with FDP politicians in the state. As a result, FDP faction-leader Hildebrandt had already stressed that they were not prepared to enter into coalition with the SPD (*HAZ*, 24 April 1990).

It should be noted that this polarisation was more a clash of personalities than policy, and was not so evident in the comparison of party programmes. For instance, the SPD's position on themes such as foreign policy, the rule of law and economic governance was much closer to the FDP (and, of course, the CDU) than it was to the Greens. In discursive terms, the election literature of the Niedersachsen Greens was nowhere near as polemical as that produced by the Berlin AL but the SPD's style still had more in common with the FDP and CDU than it did with the

Greens. As in West Berlin, the areas of potential policy agreement between the SPD and the Greens included themes such as the welfare state, societal relations, and the rights of minority groups, although significant differences between the parties remained to be resolved. For instance, in terms of societal relations, the SPD continued to be far more authoritarian than the Greens, who took a more libertarian approach. Similarly, with regard to minority rights, the SPD adopted a more pragmatic and incremental stance than the Greens.

These differences notwithstanding, there were areas of broad consensus between the two parties, in similar policy areas as those selectively emphasised in West Berlin a year earlier. Within the area of internal affairs, both favoured a more socially proactive and less authoritarian form of government compared with the Albrecht era. For instance, both parties agreed about the need to make a clearer distinction between the work of the police and the security services (*Verfassungsschutzbehörde*), and intended to enhance parliamentary control over the latter. Both parties were also broadly in agreement on the need to make more of an effort to integrate foreigners into German society and on the decentralisation of powers to local communities. With regard to gender issues, both parties were in favour of setting up a Women's Ministry, the extension of equal opportunities' legislation across the field of education and training, as well as the reduction of working hours for both men and women. Within the area of social policy, both parties favoured the extension of participation and autonomy for self-help groups, serving the physically and mentally handicapped, as well as a proposition that the state of Niedersachsen should guide a Health Reform Law through the Bundesrat.

Nevertheless, within the areas of housing and town planning, economic policies and the environment, there were differences of both style and substance. In particular, the SPD were concerned to strike a balance between the ideals of ecological modernisation and the need to maintain levels of employment and investment, whilst the Greens tended to take a more idealistic stance. This was particularly true of nuclear power and the disposal of industrial and household waste. At the time, these differences appeared to be of little significance. But as the coalition moved into mid term, the combination of a deteriorating economic situation and approaching state elections would serve to re-profile these issues in the starkest terms.

The polls going into the Niedersachsen state elections of 13 May 1990 predicted a narrow victory for the governing CDU–FDP coalition. But the actual results were quite different and a clear triumph for the SPD.

Despite Schröder's perceived failings, the SPD emerged from the state elections as the biggest party, with 44.2 per cent of the vote. This represented a modest gain of 2.1 per cent from the previous state election in 1986. The CDU lost 2.2. per cent of the vote over the previous election, becoming the second biggest party in the state with 42.0 per cent. The CDU's previous coalition partners, the FDP, maintained their 6.0 per cent vote share and became the third biggest party in the legislature. The surprise losers were the Greens, whose vote dropped from 7.1 per cent to 5.5 per cent, making them the smallest party in the 155-seat state parliament. The new distribution of seats was: SPD 71, CDU 67, FDP 9 and Greens 8 (*Statistisches Amt Niedersachsens*).

The results of the election raised a number of possibilities for the parties, given that no party had a blocking majority in the legislature. Still it was clear that any coalition that excluded the SPD would be hard to defend, given their gains in the elections. In reality, the only two likely coalitions were an SPD–FDP coalition or a Red–Green coalition. But, as already made clear by the politicians, SPD–FDP co-operation was already effectively ruled out before the election and this was reconfirmed by Hildebrandt after the results came in (*FAZ*, 16 May 1990). Therefore, although it could not be ruled out (and, indeed, Schröder did not rule it out), for the SPD, the 'FDP option' was not as attractive or plausible as that of co-operation with the Greens. The attractiveness of the Greens was enhanced as they were in no position to call the shots in any coalition negotiations. The fall in their share of the vote had been a bitter pill for the party to swallow, because it deprived them of any 'kingmaker' role within the legislature. If the SPD preferred the Greens to the FDP (which it did), it was not out of pure necessity. The Greens' leverage was reduced as a result.

Regardless of which party was to be their coalition partner, the SPD were determined to take over power by the 21 June 1990, in time to send their representatives to a session of the Bundesrat on the 22 June. For their part, the CDU was determined to prevent this happening. Gansäuer, newly re-elected as the CDU's parliamentary faction leader, stated that the CDU were determined that the first scheduled meeting of the state parliament, scheduled for 27 June, would not be brought forward to accommodate the Bundesrat session (*FAZ*, 16 May 1990). The reason why the Bundesrat meeting was so important was that it was due to debate the treaty by which the German Democratic Republic was to become part of the Federal Republic. If the CDU could not prevent the formation of a new coalition before 22 June, Schröder would become

Minister President and the SPD would have a majority in the Bundesrat when the treaty was debated.

In theory, the need to form a coalition before the Bundesrat session gave the Greens some degree of leverage with the SPD. But the situation was more complex than at first appeared. Saarland Minister President Oskar Lafontaine was the SPD's Chancellor-candidate and, under his leadership, the SPD faction in the Bundesrat had adopted an obstructional stance to the treaty process. On the one hand, Schröder's victory helped the SPD because they formed the new majority within the Bundesrat. But it was no secret that Schröder and Lafontaine were rivals. Therefore, although the Niedersachsen SPD did intend to be present at the treaty debate, if for any reason this was not possible and the CDU won the debate, this was not an unmitigated disaster for Schröder's long-term ambitions to lead the SPD. Therefore, Schröder could afford to be sanguine about the timetable for coalition talks.

The SPD and Greens both agreed that coalition negotiations should start immediately. In a press conference immediately after the election results were confirmed, the Greens' parliamentary faction leader Jürgen Trittin identified a number of areas of potential conflict, as well as stressing those policy domains where agreement was possible. There were three potential areas of conflict. These were, first, environmental policy (in particular the Greens opposition of the incineration of waste and their advocacy of waste prevention and re-cycling), second, gender politics and, third, interior policy (civil rights and the rule of law). Potential consensus areas, in Trittin's opinion, were education policy (including vocational training and the development and expansion of the Kindergarten network) and other areas of social provision (*FAZ*, 16 May 1990). Trittin demanded that the Greens receive three Ministries, assumed at the time to be Environment, Women's Issues and one more within the field of social provision. In another press conference the following day, Trittin stated that the Greens wanted to negotiate an agreement that would last the full term of government. In Trittin's view, everything was negotiable, 'as long as Schröder does not want to mess us about' (*HAZ*, 17 May 1990). Inevitably, solid proof of the SPD's good will was demanded. The areas where the Greens intended to take a hard line were energy policy and waste disposal, where Trittin insisted that the SPD must make it clear that they were not scared of coming into conflict with the Bonn government and, if necessary, fighting them in the courts. For Trittin, the rejection of the principle of nuclear energy was the benchmark of co-operation.

But the Greens' room for manoeuvre was limited. This was not only because of their poor electoral performance, but also because of the explicit link they had made in the election campaign between voting Green and co-operating with the SPD to remove the Albrecht administration. Trittin's demand for three Ministries was an opening bid, but two was possibly a more realistic aspiration. A Women's Ministry was considered to be a certainty, as was one other within the field of social provision. However, it was considered unlikely that they would get the Environment portfolio. Monika Griefahn (the leader of Greenpeace in the Federal Republic and, at that point, not a member of any political party) appeared the most likely choice of Environment Minister, supported by a Green State Secretary (*Neue Presse*, 18 May 1990, *HAZ*, 18 May 1990). Commentators agreed that the Greens would have to lower their expectations.

This downbeat mood was reflected in the run-up to the start of negotiations, on the 20 May 1990, when the Greens met for a short conference in the town of Wallenhorst. The membership were on the back foot, as a result of their poor showing in the elections, and this was reflected in the tone of the speeches. One demoralised member of the executive argued that the party had not been able to convince the electorate that they could actually change anything, whilst, at the other extreme, an executive member from Osnabrück stressed the need for the party to come out fighting in order to profile itself anew before the upcoming Federal elections. The post-election gloom was deepened by a general sense of unease at the idea of the Greens not getting the Environment Ministry in any coalition agreement. Indeed, one speaker from the floor demanded that the Greens hold out for the Economics Ministry as a quid pro quo for losing 'their' environment portfolio. This was not likely and, in his speech to the conference, Jürgen Trittin stressed that the Greens would have to accept some unpleasant political facts. He paraphrased an old quote from Adenauer and declared that the Greens and the SPD 'were condemned to a positive outcome from the negotiations' (*HAZ*, 21 May 1990).

By contrast, the mood of the Niedersachsen SPD was positively bullish. As the architect of the party's return to power after fourteen years in opposition, Schröder's stock within the SPD parliamentary faction was at its height. Schröder declared that, although he wanted immediate 'success-oriented' negotiations with the Greens (*HAZ*, 18 May 1990), these had to be within parameters established by the SPD. Not only had the SPD's vote gone up but, in the 'Green heartlands' such as the university town of Göttingen, this rise had been at the expense of the Greens themselves. It was argued in the press that the rise in the SPD vote and its distribution seemed to indicate two things. First, the voters wanted a Red–Green coalition, and, second, that by questioning the Greens' claim on the Environment portfolio Schröder's SPD could make the Greens a superfluous force within the Niedersachsen party system (*FAZ*, 23 May 1990). By arguing before coalition talks had even begun that his choice of Monika Griefahn for Environment Minister was 'non-negotiable', Schröder seemed to agree.

It was agreed beforehand that the negotiations would take place in three 'discussion circles' (*Gesprächskreise*). First, a daily preliminary meeting of the delegations before the opening of official business. Second, the official bilateral coalition negotiations between the full teams from both parties. Finally, a more focused policy-specific round of talks between the relevant specialists on each team (Jun, 1994: 197). The coalition negotiations began amid high expectations on the part of the SPD and Greens. Indeed, such was the mood of optimism that both parties made a point of using their press releases to lower the level of expectations amongst their supporters (*FAZ*, 29 May 1990). From the beginning it was clear that the two environmental themes of nuclear energy and waste disposal were to be the most contentious topics up for discussion. One of the first joint announcements of the two parties was used to issue a condemnation of the decision of the (SPD-governed) state of Nordrhein-Westfalen to allow waste to be disposed of in industrial incinerators. Whilst the SPD's preferred candidate for the Environment Ministry, Frau Griefahn, was very close to the Greens' position on this theme, there were still differences to reconcile. The SPD's stance was noticeably more pragmatic than that of the Greens, and Frau Griefahn refused to completely rule out the possibility of installing high-temperature incinerators in order to burn waste (*HAZ*, 29 May 1990). For the Greens, any form of incineration was undesirable.

With regard to social policy, both parties were broadly in agreement and negotiations went well. The shape and allocation of the planned Women's Ministry was agreed (it would go to the Greens), and the coalition even agreed that it would be desirable to adopt the GDR's relatively liberal laws on the termination of pregnancy if at all possible. In addition, it was intended that the new coalition would become far more proactive in the training and re-training of the unemployed, drug-rehabilitation projects and the promotion of self-help groups. The provision of housing would be enhanced, with 50,000 new housing units planned for 1990, of which 15,000 would be social housing (*FAZ*, 29 May 1990). Because of Niedersachsen's tight financial situation, the house building programme would be funded by diverting resources from large infrastructure projects already in the pipeline, such as the extension of the A 26 arterial road into the Emsland, the building of a tunnel under the river Weser and the extension of the port at Cuxhaven (*Neue Presse*, 31 May 1990). Finally, it was intended that the coalition would repeal the so-called 'extremist laws' (*Extremistenbeschluß*), by which individuals who were members or supporters of parties that were considered extremist were banned from the civil service (*HAZ*, 31 May 1990). Obviously, the repeal of the measure would also open the door to members of the extreme right but, for the Greens, the extremist laws were an obvious affront to their origins in the student protests of the 1960s and peace and ecology movements of the 1970s.

The coalition negotiations had soon made such good progress that their success was taken for granted by everybody, to the extent that an article in the *Frankfurter Allgemeine Zeitung* referred to 'the forthcoming Red–Green state government of Niedersachsen' (*FAZ*, 5 June 1990). Nevertheless, as the allocation of seats in the new Red–Green Cabinet became evident, many of the Greens' activists became uneasy at what they regarded as the failure of their chief negotiator Jürgen Trittin to secure more than two portfolios. At a meeting of the local party in Hannover, party members demanded a more robust stance by Trittin and his team. They still demanded the Economics Ministry as compensation for the expected loss of the Environment portfolio, whilst the more ambitious also coveted the sectors of Transport and Energy (*HAZ*, 6 June 1990). Many within the party argued that a second environmentally-related post should be created because, as one Green put it, 'we don't want ourselves to say good-bye to the area of the environment completely'. It was suggested that the new Ministry might also include planning, traffic and nature protection, and that it would be filled by Jürgen Trittin himself (*Neue Presse*, 7 June 1990).

Finally, on 7 June, the negotiations came to an end. Contrary to any hopes of the Greens' grass roots, the party had to be content with just two portfolios, in contrast to the SPD's ten. The Greens did not get the Environment portfolio, or the Economics and the proposed second Environmental portfolio. Trittin himself became Minister for Federal and European Affairs which, although not an environmentally related post, still possessed a certain degree of status and prestige. In addition to Trittin's Ministry, the Greens also received the newly created Women's Ministry and would appoint the State Secretary for both the Environment and Social Ministries. But, as predicted, all the 'blue-chip' posts remained in the SPD's hands.

In purely numerical terms, the Greens did better than the SPD in terms of the division of portfolios. The May elections had resulted in the election to the legislature of 8 Green representatives and seventy-one from the SPD and, although the Greens received only two out of the twelve Cabinet posts on offer – a ratio of legislative seats to Cabinet posts of four-to-one – the SPD ratio was just seven-to-one (*HAZ*, 8 June 1990, SPD Landesverband Niedersachsen, 1990). At first glance, this would seem peculiar given that the SPD held the political initiative because of the gains they had made at the state elections. But such an interpretation ignores the fact that although certain policy sectors, such as the Environment, held disproportionate weight for the Greens, they failed to win the portfolio during the bargaining process. In reality, the allocation of the State Secretary posts, as well as Federal and European Affairs and Women's Ministries, could not make up for the loss of what should have been their core portfolio. Thus, it was no surprise that the 'Neue Presse' described the outcome of the bargaining process as 'Schröder's success', stating that 'the soon-to-be-elected head of Government … had displayed strength and only permitted the Greens to have competence for two relatively unimportant mini-Ministries' (8 June 1990).

Internal and external constraints, staffing and expertise

As in West Berlin the previous year, the most pressing problem facing the incoming Red–Green coalition in Niedersachsen was the state's poor financial status. There were two underlying reasons for this. First, the region was dominated by agriculture and heavily reliant upon subsidies for the sector, either from Bonn or through the CAP. Federal tax reforms in the late 1980s had hit Niedersachsen hard and structural funds had not made up the short fall. Second, in the late 1970s and 1980s, the state had undergone a process of partial de-industrialisation as its declining industries (such as the shipbuilding and motor industries) either went to the wall or were rationalised. This meant that Niedersachsen suffered a fall in tax revenue coupled with a rise in demand for welfare. Around the time of the 1990 state elections, the outgoing Finance Minister announced that, for the year ending 1989, the state's finances had been in deficit to the tune of DM 1.4 billion. Since 1987 measures to reduce spending had only saved DM 140 million, despite the loss of 3,000 posts within the state civil service and public sector. In particular, staffing within the Ministries had been cut to the bone. Although it was hoped that, by 1993, the state's debts could be brought below DM 1 billion (*FAZ*, 29 June 1990), any expansion of social provision, such as the housing programme announced during the bargaining process, would be limited and at the expense of other projects.

Given that there was little scope for expansion of welfare provision, it is perhaps not surprising that the focus of the coalition was more on the issues of civil rights/constitutional protection, atomic energy, waste disposal and transport policy. The problem for the coalition was that these were potentially divisive policy areas, with only limited scope for the selected emphasis of consensual themes. For instance, both parties favoured abandoning the plans agreed by the Albrecht administration to use the sites at Gorleben and Schacht Konrad as final storage facilities for nuclear waste, but the SPD took a more cautious stance than the Greens, who were impatient to close down these facilities straight away. Similarly, whilst the Greens were hostile to any form of incineration of industrial and household waste, Environment Minister Greifahn would not rule out the possibility of developing at least one high-temperature facility.

But these difficulties lay in the future and for the time being both parties stood behind the coalition agreement. The agreement set out a relatively ambitious programme of ecological modernisation, declaring an emphasis upon 'energy conservation and efficiency as well as the promotion of alternative energy sources'. Indeed, the coalition did not regard this as purely the task of one Ministry, but rather a task that required 'joined-up policy making' (in German, a *Querschnittsaufgabe*). As in Berlin, the programme was often couched in a left-libertarian or post-materialist discourse, but when 'unpacked' still displayed a reliance upon a statist/technocratic set of policy instruments (Lees, 1999).

As soon as the details of the coalition's programme were agreed, attention turned to the subject of staffing. It was clear that the SPD (and Schröder in particular) intended to make some significant changes at the highest level of officialdom in the Niedersachsen civil service. Although the CDU had been in power since 1976, they had not undertaken a wholesale re-staffing of the civil service when it came to power in 1976. One reason for this was undoubtedly the fact that it is estimated that in 1976 80 per cent of the permanent officials were SPD members. This represented a source of expertise that any incoming party would break up at their peril. Thus, a significant raft of SPD members had flourished at all levels within the state civil service and the SPD could draw upon a great deal of in-house expertise if it so wished. The irony was that, having survived fourteen years of CDU government, some of these SPD-affiliated officials were on their own party's 'hit-list' of officials to be retired (*FAZ*,

18 May 1990)! This SPD rump within the civil service was indicative of the cosy (and consensual) relationship between the parties, the administration and the NGOs, that had developed over successive SPD- and CDU-led administrations. As was to become evident, Schröder was very much a 'new broom' with a profound suspicion of this policy-making establishment. Heads were soon to roll.

All in all, Schröder made eleven changes to existing senior positions within the civil service. The head of the Police Section was a CDU appointee and had been on Schröder's 'hit-list' prior to the election. He was replaced. In addition, the SPD made it clear that they intended to replace all of the State Secretaries in the Ministries, regardless of party membership. For instance, the SPD-affiliated head of the Niedersachsen Office for the Protection of the Constitution was replaced because he opposed the proposed liberalisation of the culture of the Interior Ministry. His successor had made his name as a data protection campaigner and was firmly on the 'New Left'. Four of the state's regional heads were also retired, including CDU members in Braunschweig and Oldenburg and an FDP appointment in Hannover. Other candidates for retirement included the Chiefs of Police in Braunschweig and Hannover, the head of the Press Office, and the head of the state delegation in Bonn. Schröder also wanted to replace the head of the state radio authority in Hannover (who was a CDU member) and the head of North German Radio (NDR). However, the last two appointments were linked to the highly politicised question of media policy and were very controversial at the time. But the NDR post was not in Schröder's fiat alone, but relied upon the co-operation of the states of Hamburg and Schleswig-Holstein (who co-owned the station with Niedersachsen).

In addition to servants of the 'Ancien Regime' being sacked or 'kicked upstairs', the new coalition proposed to create a number of new posts within the state administration. For instance, Schröder had committed himself to expanding the size and role of his own State Chancellory and wanted the new State Secretary to assume a co-ordinating role between the Minister President and individual Ministries. The Environment and Women's Ministries were particularly subject to intra- and inter-party conflict, as people jockeyed for position within the emerging new hierarchy. In such a state of flux no one was safe. Even the secretary in the Minister President's office, one Frau Petermann, received notice to quit (*FAZ*, 18 May 1990)!

For the Greens, the problem of finding sufficient staff to fill posts within the administration would put them at a considerable disadvantage during the life of the coalition. Although there was a great deal of expertise in the state (particularly in the Universities), it was not on the scale of Berlin, which had also benefited from the location of the Federal Environmental Office in the city. Compared with West Berlin, the 'issue network' (Rhodes, 1986a) in Niedersachsen was looser and more atomised. Because they did not own the Environment portfolio, even this relatively small network of environmental experts was not guaranteed access to the policy-making process. (They even failed to have a representative on the Environment Ministry's Advisory Council for Recycling and Waste Disposal (Lees, 1998).)

Schröder and Trittin, the politics and policies of the Niedersachsen coalition

With the coalition agreement finalised, Schröder was elected Minister President on 21 June 1990 with a majority of three votes in the state parliament. His was the only candidature for the post and the result was announced to sustained applause from the SPD and Green benches.

Almost immediately, the new coalition was at the centre of controversy over its decision not to attend the Bundesrat vote on the treaty between the Federal Republic and the GDR, on 22 June 1990. In retrospect, the decision was a classic example of Schröder's political pragmatism. It allowed his Green coalition partners – who were on the record as opposing the treaty – off the hook, whilst not directly defying the SPD's agreed line on the issue (no doubt with the added attraction to Schröder in that it was another tactical move in his long-standing rivalry with Oskar Lafontaine). Whatever the thinking behind the decision, it provoked a scathing editorial in the local *Hannoversche Allgemeine Zeitung*, in which it was claimed that 'the glue that holds the Red and Green together is no more than the enormous appetite for power' (*HAZ*, 22 June 1990). However, the *HAZ* journalist's opinion notwithstanding, the new administration appeared to be anything but an empty office-seeking coalition. Across a wide range of policy areas, Schröder's inaugural speech as Minister President signalled the coalition's intention to embark upon a bold and reforming political programme. In particular, Schröder singled out law and order, gender politics, environmental policy, education and training, the economy and fiscal policy as specific areas through which the coalition's record as a whole would be judged (*HAZ*, 28 June 1990).

Inevitably, the new CDU and FDP opposition parties condemned the speech. CDU parliamentary leader Jürgen Gansäuer accused Schröder of summoning up visions of a 'flowery utopia', of creating a 'paper tiger' with the coalition's planned policy on nuclear energy, and of planning to turn the state-owned radio station 'Norddeutsche Rundfunk' into 'a propaganda instrument for Red–Green ideology', whilst the SPD's allies in the communications union IG Medien unleashed a 'witch hunt' against the few journalists openly associated with the CDU within the organisation. Although FDP faction leader Hildebrandt was equally scathing in his remarks, neither he nor Gansäuer ruled out some degree of co-operation with the new coalition, given that they had a clear mandate from the electorate. Indeed, Hildebrandt signalled that the FDP would tacitly support any measures to reform state-level legislation on the powers of the police and the security services (*Neue Presse*, 29 June 1990).

Unlike the Berlin coalition, the Niedersachsen coalition was not immediately beset with problems and, after 100 days of office, opinion polls still gave the coalition a 46 per cent approval rating (*HAZ*, 2 October 1990). But it was only a matter of time before the honeymoon ended and the coalition had to make hard choices that would stretch the patience of the Green rank-and-file to the limit. Inevitably, the source of the coalition's troubles was the parlous condition of the budget. In 1990 it was already clear that, by mid term, the coalition would have to deal with a substantial budget deficit. This was estimated as being around DM 2 billion by 1992 (*Neue Presse*, 17 April 1990). As a result, the coalition would have to cut planned expenditure by a similar amount over the period. At the same time, as part of the unification process, Niedersachsen was committed to provide over 4.4. billion Marks of aid to the new Land of Saxony-Anhalt over the four years to 1994. Given the ambivalence of the Greens to the whole issue of German unification, the diversion of scarce funds to the East was highly unpopular, particularly given the growing evidence that the social safety-net in Niedersachsen was under considerable strain. For instance, a report from the highly respected 'Eduard Pestel Instituts für Systemforschung' (ISP) estimated that, in 1989, the state was already short of over 100,000 housing units and that the deficit was forecast to rise to 190,000 by 1994, mainly because of economic migration into Niedersachsen from elsewhere within the Federal Republic (*HAZ*, 16 April 1990). Obviously, much of the projected shortfall was an inevitable result of unification but Niedersachsen was also short of housing stock as a result of the policies pursued by the outgoing administration. Indeed, even a local FDP politician was forced to admit that the 'social component' of CDU–FDP policy had been neglected under Albrecht (*HAZ*, 12 April 1990).

Whoever was responsible for the housing shortage, the new coalition had to deal with the situation, even though their hands were tied for a number of reasons. For instance, given the scarcity of Federal resources following unification, the bulk of measures to address the housing crisis would have to be self-financing. The most obvious tactic would have been to initiate a steep rise in public sector rent levels in order to raise revenue that could have been invested into new housing stock, whilst at the same time restricting demand over the short to medium term, by making public sector housing less attractive. The costs of such a strategy would have obviously fallen on the most economically vulnerable sections of society and it was politically difficult for a new left-of-centre administration to adopt it. So in the short term, the problem was fudged. Indeed, a rise in public sector rents that had been agreed by the previous administration was subsequently restricted by the new coalition. In addition, it was decided that any future rent rises would be capped at no more than 30 per cent over the period up to 1995 (*HAZ*, 17 April 1990). But it was not just the housing sector that was affected by the new budgetary austerity. The new coalition had also committed itself to providing start-up funds for a programme of construction of hospital facilities throughout Niedersachsen. By 1991, eleven new hospitals under construction, involving an investment of DM 110 million of state funds, were threatened with massive delays or even cancellation because of liquidity problems (*HAZ*, 30 March 1991). As the need to save money became more apparent, it was becoming harder for individual Ministries to square the circle of available finances and manifesto commitments.

Inevitably, the debate over the coalition's first budget was bitter, with the opposition parties resisting the coalition's efforts to pin the blame on the previous administration. The centrepiece of the budget was a planned saving of DM 444 million for the following financial year. Not only were the planned cuts politically contestable in general terms, but the state government planned to achieve a significant proportion of these savings by clawing back DM 130 million of public funds normally allocated to local communities in order to offset transfers to the Eastern states. Given that the CDU and FDP were still in power in many of these communities, they took a dim view of such methods and the CDU even walked out of the negotiations, criticising Schröder's tough stance as 'defamation and dishonest demagoguery' (*HAZ*, 18 March 1991). But all parties knew that the state of Niedersachsen's finances did make depressing reading. The total 1991 budget was DM 34.2 billion, which represented an increase of DM 1.8 billion on the previous year. The budget deficit for 1991 was DM

2.4 billion, which was an increase of DM 500 million over the previous year, which meant that the total state debt was now DM 43.2 billion. The size of the debt meant that, in 1991 alone, DM 6.2 billion were needed merely to pay the interest on it. This was more than the total budget of any individual Ministry (*HAZ*, 16 March 1991).

At the same time as the state was trying to off-set some of its costs on to local communities, its Finance Minister Heinrich Swieter (SPD) was engaged in an increasingly bitter fight with Bonn over Niedersachsen's share of Federal structural funds. As already noted, Albrecht had managed to secure an annual DM 680 million of structural funds from the Federal government shortly before being voted out of office (*FAZ*, 25 February 1989). But now Bonn needed to cut back on aid to the Western states in order to fund the increasingly huge transfers to the former GDR. As a result, the DM 2.45 billion of aid earmarked for Niedersachsen up until 1988 was to be axed with only a one-off 'bridging payment' of DM 600 million to shore up the 1250 projects across the state that were dependent on the funding (*HAZ*, 6 September 1991). This led Swieter to accuse Bonn of a 'breach of trust' (*Neue Presse*, 6 September 1991). A few days later, the opposition FDP came out as unlikely allies of Swieter in his war of words with Bonn. Despite being implicated in the huge mountain of debt that the Albrecht regime had bequested to its successor, the FDP issued a sharp critique of Federal Finance Minister Theo Waigel for reneging on the promise of Federal aid. At the same time the FDP could not resist criticising the SPD and Greens for not getting spending under control (*HAZ*, 9 September 1991). If one looked at the figures, there was some truth to the FDP's criticism. In an article in the *Hannoversche Allgemeine Zeitung* reviewing the coalition's record after two years in office, it was pointed out that the coalition had enjoyed the highest gross income in the state's history (DM 6.2 billion) and still managed to generate new net debts of DM 6.6 billion. In addition, the coalition had also 'plundered' DM 1.6 billion out of the state's reserves (*HAZ*, 4 May 1992), despite the fact that many of the coalition's manifesto promises remained unfulfilled.

One of the most high profile of these promises regarded education policy. In the coalition agreement, the SPD and Greens committed themselves to, amongst other things, the creation of 600 new teaching posts, the setting up of a special fund of DM 3 million in order to promote autonomous parent–child groups, and a general expansion of education and training across the sector (SPD Landesverband Niedersachsen, 1990: 30–6). The scope of the coalition's promises reflected the fact that, as in

Berlin (and indeed the Federal Republic as a whole), the Greens were especially well represented within the educational sector and the relevant trade unions. As in Berlin, any perceived failure to deliver within the sector carried with it a heavy political price. By the summer of 1993, with less than a year before the next state elections, teachers were at the forefront of an increasingly large group of public sector workers who felt aggrieved by the failure of the coalition to improve working conditions. The cause of the conflict was the plan originally put forward by the Federal government, but taken up by state governments, to increase the working week for teachers by an hour, starting in the academic year 1994–95. The rationale for this was that, given that everyone agreed that more teaching was needed, education authorities were faced with the choice of taking on more teachers or, alternatively, making existing employees work longer to cover any shortfall. Given the relatively large social costs associated with taking on workers in the Federal Republic, the latter was considered a far more cost-effective option, even when remuneration for the extra hour was taken into account. At the same time, it was proposed by Jürgen Trittin that the status of 'civil servant' (*Beamten*) should be removed from all but a nugatory core of teachers (Niedersächsiches Ministerium für Bundes- und Europaangelegenheiten, 20 June 1993). Trittin argued that, over the long term, this would prove to be a far more effective method of saving money, as it would mean that the state budget was less exposed to the unsustainable pension commitments associated with 'Beamten' status. Under Trittin's plan, most of the state's teachers would be employed with the reduced status and rights of a 'public sector worker' (*Angestellte im Öffentlichen Dienst*).

The teachers' union GEW reacted to what they saw as an attack on their members by threatening strike action in the Autumn of 1993 and in the run-up to the state elections in 1994 (*HAZ*, 17 June 1993). In this, they were supported by the Greens' state party organisation, which issued a statement giving some support to the plan to remove Beamten status, especially if it was accompanied by the introduction of a clearly defined right to strike, but sharply criticising the plan to lengthen the working week. Although a Green himself, Trittin was criticised for failing to block the plan in Cabinet, at least until other methods for saving money had been explored (Die Grünen Landesverband Niedersachsen. Pressemitteilung Nr. 42/6/93).

The actions of the GEW and the Greens' party organisation threw down the gauntlet to the coalition and Schröder was not slow in rising to the challenge. Although the SPD made a point of setting up a consultation process with teachers' representatives across Niedersachsen, heavy briefing of journalists made it clear that the substance of the proposal was not negotiable. This prompted a rash of headlines emphasising the SPD's stand against the Greens' party organisation and their allies in the unions (for example *HAZ*, 11 September 1993, *Oldenburgische Volkszeitung*, 11 September 1993, *Achimer Kreiszeitung*, 11 September 1993, *Verdener Aller-Zeitung*, 11 September 1993, *Nordsee Zeitung*, 11 September 1993). What had started as a technical issue arising out of the poor condition of the state's finances had, in the run-up to state elections in 1994, increasingly become presented as a political trial of strength between Minister President Schröder's SPD and their junior partners the Greens, in league with their public sector allies.

The profiling of issues as intra-coalition trials of strength is a recurring theme throughout the life of the coalition. These were either related to the ecological themes (in particular the incineration of waste, waste prevention and recycling) which Trittin had presciently identified as being potentially contentious at the outset of coalition negotiations, or to industrial policy, where Schröder's stance was considerably more pro-business than the Greens. In addition, the political temperature was also raised by the fact that budgetary restraints were inhibiting overall progress, even within those areas (for example, training and schools, social welfare) where Trittin had stated that the SPD and Greens were broadly in agreement (*FAZ*, 16 May 1990).

One example of such conflict arose over the decision – taken at the beginning of 1992 – to build an incinerator for poisonous waste in Niedersachsen. On the advice of the Federal government's Technical Directorate for Waste Disposal (*Technische Anleitung Abfälle*, or TA), Niedersachsen was advised that it should build a high-temperature incinerator to dispose of waste. The main advocate of such a strategy within the coalition was SPD faction chair Johann Bruns, who stated he was 'convinced that the coalition will come to an agreement in the first half of this year to build a build a high temperature incineration facility in Niedersachsen' (*Ostfriesische Nachtrichten*, 10 January 1992). It will be recalled that the subject of incineration was a source of controversy during the process of coalition negotiations, with one of the first joint announcements of the two parties being a condemnation of the decision of the (SPD-governed) state of Nordrhein-Westfalen to allow waste to be burned in industrial incinerators. For the Greens any form of incineration was undesirable, and Bruns' declaration was greeted with dismay – although the thought that Bruns might have been deliberately provoking them into some form of over-reaction did not seem to occur to them. The same day, the Green Party Executive issued a press release condemning Bruns, stating that 'the coalition agreement clearly anticipates that priority will be given to a programme of waste avoidance, and the Greens will be pushing strongly for this over the next months'(Die Grünen Landesverband Niedersachsen, Pressemitteilung, Nr. 60/1/92). The issue illustrates how certain political themes took on a symbolic importance as a litmus test of coalition management. For instance, the dispute over the planned incinerator prompted a revealing comment by Bruns, when he declared that the first year of the coalition had been one of 'political innovation', but that now the priority had to be 'consolidation' (*Ostfriesen Zeitung* 11 January 1992). This was a signal that the SPD was tacking back towards the political centre.

No doubt this was partly in response to a sequence of electoral reverses for the SPD across North Germany. For instance, on 7 October 1991 – just a week after the Bremen SPD had suffered heavy losses in the state elections – the Niedersachsen SPD suffered a significant loss of support in the mid-term communal elections. The SPD scored 39.7 per cent, a percentage point down on the previous communal election in 1986 but 5 per cent down on their vote-share in the state elections the previous year. By contrast, the Greens polled 6.4 per cent, up a percentage point from 1986 and 1990. For the opposition parties the communal elections signalled a strong recovery, with the CDU scoring 43.9 per cent (still down from their 1986 score but up almost two percentage points on the state elections) and the FDP 6.5 per cent (up on 1986 and 1990 and higher than the Greens despite their gains) (*HAZ*, 7 October 1991). For the SPD, the results boded ill for the Niedersachsen state elections in 1994. The Social Democrats had lost support to both the CDU and the FDP, whilst the success of the Greens meant that it could not be written off as 'mid-term blues'. It was clear that the party had to regain the political initiative from both the opposition and its political allies in the coalition. In keeping with Gerhard Schröder's political instincts, the party assumed a more centrist and populist tone.

Another political theme that enabled the SPD to profile itself was the EXPO 2000 project, due to take place in Hannover's huge exhibition and conference complex. The original decision to hold the exhibition in the Niedersachsen state capital had been taken in 1989, under the previous Albrecht regime and before the collapse of the GDR. The new coalition had inherited the plan, with all the costs that came with it, but were not at one with regard to how they would proceed. Significant elements within the Greens advocated cancelling the project completely and using the money saved elsewhere. There was some merit to this argument, given the huge pressure on resources not only to finance the coalition's policy commitments, but also to fund the massive transfers to the new Eastern states. But the Greens' objections were not merely pragmatic – they were also ideological. As in Berlin, where high-profile projects were opposed by the AL, the Niedersachsen Greens' objections were also motivated by an atavistic dislike of such big capital-intensive prestige undertakings. This combination of practical and ideological objections is captured by a press statement released by the Greens' state party organisation at the beginning of 1992, which stated inter alia that 'comprehensive ecological development … is not realisable through prestige projects informed by the 'faster-higher-further ideology' (Die Grünen Landesverband Niedersachsen, Pressemitteilung, Nr. 61/1/92.). In short, the Greens wanted to cancel the EXPO and invest the resources in a programme of ecological structural development in the Eastern states.

Unlike the Greens, the SPD was torn between cancelling or continuing the EXPO. On the one hand, as in Berlin, it saw the attraction of transferring the resources to other (and more immediate) projects. There were economic benefits in going ahead as well (especially with regard to employment prospects within the construction industry), but they were more diffuse and mainly in the medium term. However, senior Social Democrats also appreciated the popularity and prestige that such projects can bring, and saw the advantages in being associated with it in the public mind. As the originators of the whole EXPO project, the CDU were also keen for EXPO to go ahead. The trick, therefore, was for the SPD to come up with a strategy that distanced itself from its coalition allies, did not allow the CDU to claim a victory either and, most importantly, allowed the party to keep its options open. The answer was a referendum of the citizens of Hannover on the subject of whether there should be an EXPO in their city. Under pressure from the SPD – and against the wishes of its state executive – the Greens in the parliamentary faction grudgingly accepted the idea of a referendum as a way out of what had become an impasse. The idea had the added attraction for the state government because it was ostensibly taking place at the city government level in Hannover, which allowed them to distance themselves from the process. Given that he was on record as being opposed to such referenda, Gerhard Schröder wasted little time in distancing himself, declaring that, although he was not disturbed by the prospect of such a referendum, it 'was not really his theme, but something for which the communal politicians in

Hannover had to be held responsible' (*HAZ*, 16 January 1992). The referendum was arranged for some time in the first two weeks of the July of 1992.

The SPD's strategy worked on two levels, both of which served to shore-up moderate support amongst the voters of Niedersachsen. First, the logistics of the EXPO went ahead, including a promise of financial support from the Federal Government in Bonn, as part of a framework agreement on the exhibition. This was a triumph for Schröder as the 'Father of the state' (*Landesvater*), especially so as, only the previous December, Finance Minister Theo Waigel had cast doubt on the possibility of an aid package from the Federation (*HAZ*, 2 December 1991). Second, it served to distance the SPD from the abstentionist stance of the Greens. At their state party conference in Hildesheim at the end of March 1992, the Greens' grass roots reacted in predictable fashion. A motion from the floor rejecting the whole idea of EXPO 2000, on the grounds of it being contrary to the coalition agreement, was passed unanimously (*Nordsee Zeitung*, 30 March 1992). The conference also rejected Johann Bruns' plan for a high-temperature incinerator, which was still a highly contentious issue within the coalition. Indeed, what is noticeable about press reports from this period of the coalition is the degree to which the two issues were cited by the Greens as evidence of the treachery of the SPD, with calls for a withdrawal from the coalition. This was resisted by the more realistic members of the Greens, such as Chairperson Thea Dückert, who pleaded that it would be 'foolhardiness' to risk the coalition on the resolution of one issue (*HAZ*, 31 March 1992). But the fact that the issue of continuing the coalition was already so openly discussed was evidence of the process of distancing between the two parties as state elections drew near.

On the national stage, however, Minister President Schröder was still an enthusiast for the whole concept of Red–Green political co-operation. This was in marked contrast to Walter Momper, whose experiences in Berlin had left him bitter and disillusioned with the Greens. Momper had gone as far as to call the Red–Green coalition an 'exhausted model', a phrase that was picked up and used by CDU politicians in Niedersachsen (*HAZ*, 5 May 1993). The differences in the two approaches was partly a reflection of the comparatively successful process of coalition maintenance in Niedersachsen, and the lack of personal animus between the main players. But Schröder's continuing advocacy of the Red–Green project coincided with a period of speculation that he might be adopted as the SPD's Chancellor-candidate, following the resignation of Bjorn Engholm in 1993.[2] In this context, the continued success of the coalition was an asset, especially given that it was generally accepted within the SPD that the party had to find new sources of electoral support if it was to have any hope of returning to Bonn as the senior member of the Federal Government. In an interview with the down-market tabloid *Neue Presse*, Schröder stated that 'the toppling of the Kohl government ... is only possible in a Red–Green constellation' (4 May 1993).

It was clear that Schröder was not speaking for the national SPD at the time. However, within a day of his interview it was apparent that his opinion was not even universally held within his own party in Niedersachsen, when state party Chair Johann Bruns issued a press statement criticising any 'commitment' by Schröder to a Red–Green coalition at the national level, saying that it 'wasn't very helpful' (*HAZ*, 5 May 1993). Bruns' comments are interesting for two reasons. First, it gives one an insight into the nature of intra-party power relationships in the Niedersachsen SPD. What is clear from this is that Schröder was under pressure from elements within his own party who were not as relaxed about co-operating with the Greens as he was. Second, it casts light on inter-party power relationships within the coalition. In particular, Bruns' provocation of the Greens over the matter of the high-temperature reactor and the need to make 1992 'a year of consolidation' begin to appear to be part of a pattern of resistance to both Schröder as a coalition manager, and the Greens as coalition partners.

Of course the Greens had their own share of resistors. At their state party conference in June 1993 at Osnabrück, the Greens launched a number of bitter attacks on their coalition partners, particularly Schröder and Monika Griefahn. These attacks were immediately dismissed by the SPD as nothing more than early electoral manoeuvring on behalf of the Greens (*HAZ*, 8 June 1993). Yet this was not really the case, given that the attacks covered a wide range of coalition policies, including the environment, asylum policy and schooling, and were primarily from the Greens' grass roots, who were far more concerned with Green shibboleths than with acquiring an early electoral advantage. Indeed, prominent politicians from the Green parliamentary faction were relatively positive about the coalition, with Trittin in particular echoing Schröder's claim that only a Red–Green coalition could topple Kohl's government in Bonn (*HAZ*, 7 June 1993).

Although both sides were still keen to continue the coalition, by the time of the Osnabrück conference politicians of every ideological colour were becoming increasingly pre-occupied with the forthcoming elections in 1994. In the Federal Republic, it was going to be a busy year of state and local elections (seventeen in all), culminating in the European elections in June and the national elections to the Bundestag in October. As a result, 1994 was already known as 'super election year' (*Superwahljahr*), with the more senior Niedersachsen politicians – and especially Schröder – expecting to play a major role in at least three elections. The first hurdle was the state elections on 13 March and, in consequence, the analysis of opinion polling of the state's electorate took on a new importance.

It has to be remembered that the 1994 election would be fought under somewhat different economic circumstances to that of 1990. While the 1990 elections were fought at the top of the economic cycle (which the immediate aftermath of the collapse of the GDR had stoked up into a national economic boom), the 1994 elections were to be fought in the midst of a recession. Given the more straightened economic circumstances, the public mood had shifted away somewhat from 'post- materialist' themes towards 'bread and butter issues' such as unemployment. But polling showed that politicians of the left had to steer a fine line between materialist and post-materialist concerns. For instance, a six-month time series analysis of opinion in Niedersachsen, carried out in the first half of 1993 by a private polling organisation, showed that unemployment was identified as the biggest problem facing the state, with 17 per cent of those polled citing it. Within the total, it was clear that blue-collar workers (23 per cent) and/or SPD voters (20 per cent) were most likely to identify it as the biggest problem. On the other hand, there seemed to be a clear tendency across almost all social groups towards pessimism when asked if they expected their own economic circumstances to get better or worse over the next year (with a ratio of more than 2:1 amongst blue-collar workers). However, the next most important issue was still the environment (7 per cent), followed by the economy (6 per cent, but with an upward trend towards the end of the series), the asylum issue and politics in general (5 per cent), the housing crisis (4 per cent), EXPO 2000 and fear of foreigners (3 per cent). But the most striking thing – and this is highlighted in the executive summary to the poll report – was the huge number of those polled who said there was no problem that they could think of (39 per cent)! Such a large amount of essentially satisfied (or apathetic) voters was also reflected in generally good approval ratings for Schröder and the coalition parties. For instance, Schröder's approval ratings (ranked along a scale from +5 to –5) stayed in the positive throughout the period, with his approval rating double that of his new CDU rival Christian Wulff. Finally, the SPD led the CDU by a clear margin (47 per cent to 34 per cent), with the Greens (9 per cent) well ahead of the FDP (5 per cent). Moreover, the SPD's popularity compared with that of the CDU grew over the course of the series (FORSA, Gesellschaft für Sozialforschung und statistiche Analysen mbH, 1993: 1–14).

Given these polling figures, the coalition appeared to be in a good position to fight the next state elections. Nevertheless, if one was a Green strategist, one might be forgiven for wishing that the SPD was a little less popular. A politician as shrewd as Schröder could not help but realise that, given a fair wind, 47 per cent of the vote could well deliver the Niedersachsen SPD a working majority in the state parliament. This was because the 5 per cent electoral barrier might, on the strength of these opinion poll figures, deny the FDP any seats in the new legislature. This would leave three parties (the SPD, CDU and Greens) in the legislature. Given that a coalition between the CDU and Greens was unlikely to say the least, the SPD might be able to govern alone if the sums added up on election night. But the election was still a year away, and the SPD still had a lot of work to do in order to secure such a majority. Given that it would be hard to imagine the CDU's support being driven down any further, any further political capital would quite conceivably have to be won at the expense of the Greens.

One can only speculate as to what calculations were made by the parties in the run-up to the 1994 elections. Nevertheless, what is clear is that the last year of the coalition was characterised by a rash of intra-coalition disputes which served to profile those areas of policy which had the potential to be contentious. To some extent they all carried an ideological charge, with a (sometimes explicit) trade-off between quality-of-life issues such as the environment and so-called 'bread and butter issues'.

The common approach to environmental policy began to unravel in October 1993, when Schröder officially approved the so-called 'Europipe' project. The project involved the laying of a gas pipeline from the North Sea Oil and Gas fields to the Federal Republic. The project was to be built by the Norwegian Shipping Engineering Company Statoil, who planned to invest DM 3.3 billion into the project. Such a huge investment would have a beneficial effect on the depressed local economy of the North Sea coast and beyond. However, the project had been resisted by the Greens on ecological grounds, not least that the pipeline ran through the 'Nationalpark Wattenmeer', a unique and delicate habitat of mud flats. The pipeline was planned to come on-line in October 1995. Although the actual decision was taken by a local planning office in the small town of

Claustal-Zellerfeld, no-one doubted that Schröder had a hand in the decision. As Gila Altmann, the Greens' press spokesperson, put it, 'it has nothing to do with a bureaucratic act by an office, but is rather about the political will of the Minister President – it is a black day for environmental politics in Niedersachsen' (Bündnis 90/Die Grünen Landesverband Niedersachsen Geschäftsstelle, Pressemitteilung, Nr. 85/10/93.).

Two other thorns of contention were the 'Eurofighter' debate and a scandal over an atomic reactor at Stade. The Eurofighter row arose because of a conscious decision to support the policy of securing jobs in Niedersachsen, through such pump-priming measures as supporting the role of the DASA in the defence project. Although the Daimler-Benz aerospace division had a factory in the town of Lemwerder, which was threatened with closure, the idea of using state funds to support such a project enraged the Greens. For the SPD, such high-tech projects were essential in order to maintain Niedersachsen's industrial base, but for many in the Greens such projects represented the military-industrial complex at its worst. Around the same time, a decision was taken by Environment Minister Griefahn to cut short the safety audit of the nuclear power station at Stade, rather than shut it down as originally envisaged in the coalition agreement. Coming on the heels of the Eurofighter row, this only served to rub salt into the wound and was taken as a signal that the SPD was deliberately trying to provoke its coalition partners. Although the Greens were aware that the SPD had more coalition options than they, attitudes began to harden as a result. In an interview with the magazine *Bild* in November 1993, Andrea Hoops, nominated the Greens' leading figure for the upcoming elections, pointed out that despite the obvious successes of the coalition (45,000 new nursery places, 60,000 new flats, etc.), there was a limit to the party's patience with their Social Democratic allies. 'We are not going to run after the SPD!', she declared (*Bild*, 22 November 1993).

The Greens' state party conference in Aurich that month allowed the grass roots to voice their displeasure at these projects. The Eurofighter project was particularly resented, with calls for the project to be cancelled and the money spent on developing more environmentally friendly forms of civil aviation. With regard to the Stade nuclear reactor, delegates pinned the blame for the reversal of policy squarely on Monika Griefahn. Rage at Griefahn now had an added venom, given that she was no longer ostensibly independent from either party, but had joined the SPD. What the Greens regarded as political disappointments in the environmental field, such as within the fields of nuclear policy and waste disposal, were laid fairly and squarely at the door of their Social Democratic allies (*Süddeutsche Zeitung*, 22 November 1993, *TAZ*, 22 November 1993).

Schröder was not slow in responding in kind to these attacks. The following day, he gave an interview to the *HAZ*, in which he declared that Greens 'did not understand how serious the economic crisis was' and that the SPD was only prepared to co-operate with politicians whose first priority was the preservation of jobs. As a result, Schröder declared, the SPD now regarded the continuation of the coalition after the March elections as the second-best option. For the SPD, the aim was now to win an absolute majority in the state parliament (*HAZ*, 23 November 1993). This was taken up by SPD Chair Bruns, who said that, in his opinion, the Greens had not been able to reconcile their instinct for fundamentalist opposition with what he called the 'urge for office and political influence'. Although he saw no alternative to the coalition before the state elections, Bruns also stated his preference for an absolute majority for the SPD in the next legislative period (*Braunschweiger Zeitung*, 23 November 1993).

The gloves were now off and the Greens found themselves on the receiving end of some sustained criticism. Underlying this debate was the feeling that the Greens were not able to come to terms with the new realities of post-unification Germany, particularly the more straightened economic circumstances. If any future coalition with the Greens was to take place, the SPD demanded a new realism on the part of their partners. In an interview with the *HAZ* the following month, Johann Bruns stated that the Greens would have to accept that the preservation and creation of jobs sometimes took precedence over environmental considerations. He pointed to the long litany of projects that the Greens had opposed over the life of the coalition. These included the Europipe project, a Mercedes test-track at Papenburg which Schröder had personally ensured had been transferred from Baden-Württemberg to Niedersachsen, and the dredging of the river Ems in order to make it deep enough for the super-liner Oriana to pass through after it was built. Bruns declared that the Greens would have to accept that projects of this type would inevitably take place in the future, because economic policy was going to be the most important task in the next few years and the SPD would only co-operate with those who were prepared to help (*HAZ*, 16 December 1993). Others went further than even Bruns was prepared to go in criticising the Greens. The previous month, an editorial in the same paper had suggested that a Grand Coalition was more desirable than a continuation of the Red–Green option, because Schröder and CDU faction leader Gansäuer both understood the need to preserve the state's industrial base. The editorial scorned the antics of the Greens' grass roots at their conference a few days earlier, stating that 'the Greens have simply already excluded themselves from the coalition as a serious partner' (*HAZ*, 25 November 1993).

It was clear that the Greens were in deep political trouble and, as the new year came around, polls still put the SPD on course for a possible majority after the state elections in the Spring. By contrast, the Greens were doing badly in the polls and looked set to lose support. In January 1994, the Greens' Andrea Hoops undertook a series of interviews with the press, in which she defended the Greens' record in government and set out their stall for the elections and beyond. She stated that the presence of the Greens had 'added some backbone and innovation' to the coalition, observing that, for instance, nearly all the legal frameworks which governed such areas as education, nature protection, policing and the security and intelligence services had been reformed over the course of the coalition. However she professed to be unhappy with the record of Monika Griefahn's Environment Ministry and saw the issuing of that portfolio to the Greens as the benchmark of any future coalition with the SPD. Hoops went even further, stating that the Greens' main task for the state elections was preventing the SPD from gaining an absolute majority, thus preventing Schröder from nurturing his 'authoritarian style' still further over the next four years (*Cellesche Zeitung*, 28 January 1994, Bild, 2 February 1994).

For all her fighting talk, Hoops was not arguing from a position of strength. Not only was her party languishing in the polls, but the parliamentary faction itself was now split between those who wanted to continue co-operating with the SPD and those who wanted to embark on a more confrontational course. Even those Greens who had been well-disposed towards the SPD now realised that the SPD had manoeuvred them into an impossible position. Jürgen Trittin was on record as saying that Schröder's emphasis on bread and butter issues, which had started the previous autumn, was more than just a political tactic in the run-up to the election but was rather a profound change of emphasis, especially on the part of Gerhard Schröder. Trittin had spent much of the last four years defending Schröder, Griefahn and the Red–Green coalition in general against the more paranoid suspicions of the Greens' grass roots, but now he said defiantly that 'the biggest enemy of the Red–Green Land government is the Minister President' (*HAZ*, 19 February 1994). For all intents and purposes, the coalition was at an end.

On Sunday the 13 March 1994, the citizens of Niedersachsen went to the polls to elect a new state parliament. The SPD polled 44.3 per cent of the vote, giving them 80 of the 159 seats (an overall majority of one). The Greens did better than expected, polling 7.4 per cent (up almost 2 per cent on their 1990 showing). The CDU was down almost six percentage points at 36.4 per cent, whilst the FDP (4.4 per cent) failed to enter the new legislature (Statistisches Amt Niedersachsens). Schröder's instincts had been proved correct and he was now firmly entrenched as Niedersachsen 'Landesvater'. His coalition had survived the full term through some difficult economic circumstances and, despite intra-party conflicts, both coalition partners had improved their vote share at the expense of their opponents on the right. Nevertheless, the Greens were now consigned to the opposition benches, having failed in their stated objective of preventing the SPD gaining an absolute majority.

Having endured so much criticism from a Green party that regarded the Environment portfolio as theirs by right, the last word must go to Monika Griefhan. At 18.50 hours on Sunday 13 March, with the exit polls indicating an SPD victory, she turned to a journalist working for the *Neue Presse* and declared that 'the SPD can also make very good Green policy without the Greens' (*Neue Presse* 14 March 1994). For Griefahn in particular, victory must have tasted sweet indeed.

Notes

1   The Emnid poll put Albrecht on 55 per cent and Schröder on 36 per cent. Moreover, as one of the most extrovert of the so-called 'Toscana socialists' within the SPD, Schröder's personal style appeared to aggravate the traditionally dour citizens of Niedersachsen. For instance, SPD voters polled objected to his 'dramatic' manner. Moreover, on a 1–5 sympathy rating, Schröder only scored 1.63 amongst SPD supporters. Bearing in mind that this was only marginally ahead of the 1.56 scored by the CDU's Rita Süssmuth (the Bundestag speaker and designated successor to Albrecht as Minister President if the CDU returned to power), it indicated that, at that time, Schröder's personality was perceived to be a political problem.

2   Following Oskar Lafontaine's failure o unseat Helmut Kohl in the 1990 Bundestag elections, Engholm became SPD leader and provisional Chancellor-candidate in 1991. However, revelations that he had lied over aspects of the 'Barschel affair' in Schleswig-Holstein forced Engholm to stand down from this position. He was replaced by Rudolf Scharping and is no longer a major figure within the SPD.

6

Party strategy and the 1998 Bundestag elections

Schröder and Lafontaine: solving the SPD's 'chancellor question'

In the 1972 Bundestag elections, the SPD polled 45.8 per cent of the vote and became the biggest party in the new parliament (Padgett, 1993). This was to prove to be the high point of its post-war performance and, since then, it has been in both electoral and ideological decline. This decline accelerated in the 1980s and 1990s, following the collapse of the Social–Liberal coalition in 1982 and, during this time, the Social Democrats fielded four unsuccessful candidates for Chancellor, losing four Bundestag elections in a row and suffering a steady erosion in support in their 'core' states. This decline reached its apogee in 1995, in the Berlin state elections of 22 October. The SPD lost 6.6 per cent across the city, with their vote share dropping by 4 per cent in the Western half and a devastating 12.1 per cent in the East. As a result, the SPD was no longer the strongest party in any district of Berlin. In the East, it had been the strongest party but now lay behind both the PDS and the CDU. In the West, it even slumped to 29.8 per cent in its once rock-solid heartland of Wedding it was also beaten by the Greens in the bohemian districts of Kreuzberg and Mitte 01. Bearing in mind that under Willy Brandt in 1963 the Berlin SPD scored 62 per cent of the vote, it is not too strong to describe the SPD's 1995 performance as a humiliation. It was certainly their worst-ever performance in Berlin and provoked speculation as to the SPD's long-term future as a catch-all party (cf. Lees, 1996: 63–72). The Berlin result was analogous with the Labour party's disastrous 1983 General Election defeat. Obviously the Berlin election was restricted to one state, but – like the Labour party's experience in 1983 – the sheer scale of the erosion of the SPD's core vote cast doubts upon its future as an alternative party of government. Thus many observers expected the Berlin meltdown to provoke a comprehensive re-evaluation of the SPD's strategy along the lines of what had taken place within the Labour party in the 1980s.

In the event these observers were only half right. The Berlin result was fatal for Rudolf Scharping, the party leader at the time, who was ousted by Oskar Lafontaine at the SPD annual conference the following month. In the next two and a half years Lafontaine turned the party around, at least in terms of self-confidence. What Stephen Silvia memorably described as the 'loosely coupled anarchy' (Padgett, 1993: 171) of the late 1980s and early 1990s was replaced by a steelier approach to the business of opposition.

Superficially at least, Lafontaine can be regarded in this respect as the SPD's equivalent of Neil Kinnock. Like Kinnock, Lafontaine was on the left of his party when he came to power and very quickly established an iron grip on the party machine, making it a much more formidable political competitor to the CDU. But whereas Neil Kinnock's efforts to reform the Labour party involved jettisoning what were perceived as unpopular policies and incrementally narrowing the ideological distance between Labour and the Conservatives, Lafontaine's political strategy was to sharpen the political debate and offer a more confrontational and explicitly left-wing stance. In particular, the SPD's majority in the Bundesrat was used ruthlessly to undermine the Federal government's legislative programme and profile the SPD. In addition to his control of the Bundesrat, Lafontaine's position as Minister President of Saarland gave him a real power-base with which to take on the Federal Government. Lafontaine's faith in his own ability to do this was reflected in his keynote speech to the SPD's national conference in Hannover at the beginning of December 1997. His position as darling of the conference was never in doubt and the speech was a red-blooded re-affirmation of the Social Democratic project, advocating state intervention to secure social justice, more regulation, 'green' taxes and greater European integration as a bulwark against the forces of globalisation. This was a formula that he had already put into practice in his home state where, interestingly, it had served to successfully contain the local Green party. Lafontaine's robust left-wing stance had narrowed the ideological space available to the Greens on the SPD's left and they had difficulties mobilising the left-libertarian vote to the same degree as they had done in other states.

The other significant speech at the party was made by Gerhard Schröder. Whilst Lafontaine advocated state intervention and regulation, taxes and European integration, Schröder advocated flexibility and deregulation, trimming social costs and a more cautious approach to

Europe. With such sentiments, Schröder was easily cast in the role of a Blair-type 'moderniser', whose job was to drag the SPD kicking and screaming into the twenty-first century. Like Blair he had a deeply ambivalent attitude towards the traditions and values of his own party and – demonstrated during his career in Niedersachsen – had a similar gift for tapping into the concerns of the general public and articulating them in a populist manner.

The analogue with Blair was further enhanced by Schröder's obvious popularity with the general public, especially compared with Lafontaine. For despite Lafontaine's obvious political strengths and high regard within the party, all of the opinion poll data at the turn of the year indicated that he would fail once more to unseat Kohl, or his putative successor Wolfgang Schäuble. Schröder by contrast enjoyed an opinion poll lead over Kohl of 57 per cent to 33 per cent and over Schäuble of 49 per cent to 44 per cent (*Der Spiegel*, 20 December 1997). Because of this, many observers assumed that Schröder was the obvious choice for Chancellor-candidate. It was recognised that he was distrusted within his own party (despite his power base as Minister President of Niedersachsen), but so was Blair, and the similarities between Schröder and the recently triumphant British Prime Minister gave his candidacy a formidable momentum.

But closer observers of the German political system recognised that in reality Schröder had to play his hand carefully. It was clear that his popularity in the country was based upon his centrist stance as moderniser, but conversely if he was to beat Lafontaine to the nomination he could not afford to create too much ideological distance between himself and the party membership. To borrow a phrase from the Clinton campaigns, he had to 'triangulate' between the two positions of the activists and the wider populace (Lees, 1998). At the same time, the lack of an internal competitor on the left meant that Lafontaine had the freedom to edge towards the centre ground. This would have left Schröder with two strategic options. First, he could tack further to the centre himself, which opened up the possibility of alienating the party rank-and-file. Second, he could resist that temptation and appeal to the membership, but potentially lose the quality that made him popular with the voters – his ideological distance from the SPD's apparatchiks. Either option had its risks.

In the end, Schröder placed all his bets on a handsome win in the state elections in Niedersachsen on 1 March 1998. For months Schröder had stated that if he did not at least hold on to his previous share of just over 44 per cent of the vote he would not stand for the nomination. At the time the pledge was made the SPD had suffered another bad electoral set-back in Hamburg and as a result Lafontaine went along with Schröder's stance, no doubt calculating that an improvement on Schröder's impressive 1994 result was unlikely. But, in doing so, Lafontaine made it very difficult to keep his own candidature open should Schröder get the result he wanted. Following the Niedersachsen SPD's resounding win in the 1 March elections, Lafontaine had to back down and give Schröder a clear run at Kohl. Central to this campaign was idea of the 'New Centre' (*Neue Mitte*), a variation on the New Democrat/New Labour strategy of 'big tent' politics. The SPD intended to build an electoral coalition that would occupy the centre ground whilst leaving open the possibility of coalition with the Greens.

Fischer and Trittin: the Greens torn between the head and the heart

But the Greens still had to demonstrate that they were suitable coalition partners at the Federal level. The 'Red–Green model' of political co-operation that had emerged over the years at state level relied upon the selective emphasis of 'quality of life' issues and the relative under-emphasis of those policy areas where the SPD and Greens disagreed, such as Defence and Foreign policy. As a result, the Greens had not been forced fully to reconsider their stance on such issues, with the result that many of the issues had become strongly embedded as articles of faith. Thus, although the heat may had gone out of the 'realo-fundi' debate of the 1980s, the Greens still possessed the capacity for internecine strife when discussing these fundamental ideological issues. This capacity was aggravated by the strong influence the grass-roots membership still exercised through the party conference. As a result, for many years the more pragmatic senior politicians, such as Joschka Fischer, had expressed their misgivings about the central role of conference in drawing up a realistic policy programme that was acceptable to both the voters and potential coalition partners.

Ranged against Fischer were those who, for ideological or personal reasons, were unwilling to move any further towards the political centre. The key figure amongst these institutional resistors was former Niedersachsen faction leader Jürgen Trittin. One will never know how much of Trittin's stance was the result of ideological conviction, rivalry with Fischer, or bitterness towards Gerhard Schröder as a result of his experiences during the 1990–94 Niedersachsen coalition. But Trittin, as the party's national spokesperson, was in a position to slow the process of programmatic reform that was required if the Greens were to be a serious contender for national government. Thus, in October 1997 Trittin announced the party's draft programme for the upcoming Bundestag elections, to be voted on by delegates to the Greens' national conference in March 1998. The draft programme was an explicit re-affirmation of Green beliefs which, by advocating the immediate withdrawal from the use of nuclear energy and the disbanding of NATO, made very few concessions to the need for ideological moderation. As such it drew immediate criticism from both within the Greens and from the SPD. Joschka Fischer took the 'realo' position that what he called 'unrealistic demands' would hamper any post-election coalition negotiations, whilst the SPD flatly rejected the draft programme as a basis for negotiations. After much debate the draft programme was re-drafted and the NATO commitment was downgraded to a long-term goal for Germany and her allies rather than a unilateral act to be taken at once. This left the road clear for the SPD to praise the new draft programme, with Federal Secretary General Müntefering telling a radio talk-show that the ditching of the anti-NATO stance 'spelled good news' for the Social Democrats (de-news@listserv.gmd.de 14 October 1997, 16 December 1997, 22 October 1997). But the ideological tussle continued. In March 1998 the Greens' national conference voted against German participation in 'S-FOR' in Bosnia, as well as proposing the eventual dissolution of NATO and steep rises in the price of petrol (amounting to 300 per cent over ten years) in order to reduce emissions of greenhouse gasses. Later that month the majority of the Bundestag parliamentary faction abstained or voted against the treaty on NATO enlargement and then one Green parliamentarian went on record suggesting that Germans should restrict themselves to one air journey every five years. The cumulative effect of these actions was to give the impression to both voters and potential partners that the Greens' impossibilist tendency was more in the ascendant and the Greens' poll ratings quickly halved from 10 per cent to around 6 per cent (Green, 1999). It seemed as if the Greens were hell-bent on scaring off moderate voters.

However, the ideological turbulence that afflicted the Greens at the start of 1998 should not be taken at face value. It has always been a feature of election campaigns that parties try and profile themselves against each other in order to mobilise their core support. The problem parties face is doing this without alienating the wider electorate. This problem is particularly acute where parties are competing for votes from within a particular social group. German political scientists have estimated the Greens' 'core' potential electorate to be around 5 per cent of total voters. In addition they identify an additional 'fringe' electorate of around 8 per cent of voters, of which they could perhaps count on about a third consistently voting Green (Raschke, 1993). The rest of this group is open to competition from the SPD and, to a lesser extent, the PDS. Therefore the Greens needed to reach beyond their core support and mobilise voters from with this part of the electorate. It was no surprise therefore to find that the substance of the Greens' electoral programme did not live up to the image of ideological purism which, for their own different reasons, was being projected by the press, competing parties, and even the Greens' own spokespeople and activists. As will become apparent, the programme had much in common with the SPD's programme or even, in parts, the CDU and FDP. Programmatically, the Greens have become a mainstream party.

Campaign strategy

The Greens' campaign for the 1998 Bundestag elections was their most professional to date, notwithstanding the early gaffes described above. The most striking change from previous years was the party's slick new artwork, including a new logo based upon the umlaut u (ü) in their name. Like much of the party's anti-party past, the familiar sunflower logo had been deemed insufficiently voter-friendly and dumped. But the Greens' new professional approach was still reassuringly old-fashioned compared with the SPD's campaign, which is widely regarded to have been the slickest and most media-oriented in the history of the Federal Republic. It was also one of the most empty and vacuous. But the campaign was effective, both in terms of organisation and strategy, and drew heavily upon the lessons of the British Labour Party's campaign the previous year.[1] Campaign organisation stressed the idea of co-ordination and lines of command between three main project teams dealing with specific themes. These teams were first, agency polling, second, rapid rebuttal (*Gegner Beobachtung*), and finally, a special working group for the Eastern states (*Arbeitsgruppe Ost*).

The agency polling team concentrated upon monitoring the work of the SPD's partner agencies with focus groups and reported back to party headquarters. It was their job to make sure that the campaign used only 'positives' and that the SPD did not use anything in the campaign that offended voters. In the parlance of the Clinton campaign, they 'watched the numbers'. Rapid rebuttal complemented this by making sure that any 'negatives' about the SPD did not become entrenched within the news cycle. This normally entailed countering stories put forward by the other parties. It also occasionally meant spinning against members of their own campaign if they went 'off-message'. The most notable victim of this aspect of their work was Jost Stollmann (Schröder's economics advisor at the time, but not an SPD member) when he began to talk too explicitly about the need for supply-side reforms of the labour market in the last week of the campaign. Finally, the Eastern working group was tasked with tailoring the SPD's overall message to voters in the new states. Because of its previously dismal showing in the East, the SPD was painfully aware that its understanding of the Eastern German voters' thinking was tenuous at best. SPD membership in the East was very low in both absolute terms and in terms of organisational density. As a result they lacked the local intelligence which established parties normally take for granted and were worried that elements of the campaign that worked well in the West might be counter-productive in the East. 'Arbeitsgruppe Ost' consisted of members who had grown up and been socialised into the Eastern German political culture. Their job, in effect, was to weed out anything that Easterners might consider to be parochial or irrelevant to their needs.

All three teams worked with the SPD's partner agencies, dealing with the marketing and advertising. There were eight of these in all, looking after different elements of the campaign. First, there were two 'creative' agencies, who were responsible for the broad ideas that underpinned the campaign, whilst a third agency was responsible for the dissemination of the campaign to the media. Once the campaign was up and running, the SPD employed another agency to poll target voters and assess its impact upon them. The results of these private polls were then given to a team of media analysts, who monitored and refined the campaign in the light of these data. The SPD also employed a number of consultancies to ensure that the party machine itself operated smoothly. One company was responsible for training of party personnel, another had overall control of the organisation and marketing of party events, and all speeches were prepared and disseminated by yet another agency. Finally, the entire operation was co-ordinated through a secure 'intra-net' network of over two thousand users by another specialist agency.

The campaign strategy was based upon four 'positives' associated with the SPD that had become apparent in pre-election polling. These were: the idea of 'political change', 'leadership', 'innovation' and 'justice'. Bundled together, these four positives were meant to add up to what the pollsters called an aura of 'future competence'. In practice, it meant concentrating upon policy areas where the SPD was perceived to be strong, such as labour market regulation, social and health provision, family life and youth. It also meant winning back a reputation for economic competence that was lost in the late 1970s and early 1980s. The SPD managed to do this and were ahead of the CDU/CSU on economic competence for most of 1998. Ominously, however, the CDU/CSU regained the initiative in this area in the last few weeks of the poll, which added to the feeling that the election result would be very close.

The most interesting theme in the SPD's campaign was the use of the phrase 'innovation' and the thinking that underpinned it. The use of the phrase dates back to 1996, at a time when the SPD was still behind in the polls. When focus groups were asked what they associated with the SPD, it became clear that a major problem was that the SPD was regarded as being resistant to change and a defender of big producer interests. At the same time, it was also evident that the word 'reform' also carried big negatives. This was because voters had come to take Germany's generous social provisions for granted, and the limited reforms that had been carried out since the early 1980s had been attempts to cut back on welfare spending. Thus 'reform' had become an ambivalent phrase in the minds of voters and was also a euphemism for cut. How voters reacted to it depended upon how they were questioned. When asked a generalised question about the need for change in the Federal Republic the voters answered in a socio-tropic manner, claiming that Germany needed to make big changes and that they were willing to vote for a party that would make such changes. Thus on the surface it appeared that the SPD's perceived failure to back reform was making them unpopular. However, when questioned more closely about their own circumstances, the voters' declared willingness to change became more ambivalent and self-interest more apparent. In other words, the pollsters had uncovered a classic free-rider problem, in which voters recognised that the future prosperity of the country depended on reform but were unwilling on a personal level to make the sacrifice. Therefore, the trick for campaign experts was to pick up the positives associated with change without the negatives. Polling indicated that 'innovation' was the phrase that fitted, and it was to be heard continuously for the two years up to polling day.

The SPD's sophisticated use of polling inevitably generated a campaign of more style than substance, and the party's determination to avoid alienating potential voters meant that they were never forced to resolve their ideological dilemma. Indeed, expectations of a close election result and the uneasy compromise struck between Schröder and Lafontaine meant that it was forced to keep its options open. But this only served to aggravate the party's ambivalent stance, spanning the materialist/post-materialist ideological divide. In fact it could be argued that the Social Democrats appeared to be torn, between not just two but three strategies. First, the party continued to court the Greens and its post-materialist supporters by emphasising those elements of their programme that were closest to the policies of the Greens. No pre-election promises were made of course, but it was clear that on issues such as the environment, gender and citizenship the two parties were reasonably close. Second, many in the party still hankered after the traditional social democratic agenda of redistribution and social justice. This tendency was strongest within the party's activists, who regarded Oskar Lafontaine as their champion within the party elite. Although Lafontaine had stood down in favour of Schröder earlier in the year, he was clearly intent on wielding power behind the scenes and was not afraid of making public his beliefs. Although on many issues – such as eco-taxes – the Lafontaine wing of the party was very close to the Greens, they retained a strong statist and producer-interest orientation that was in direct conflict with a post-materialist agenda. More thoughtful members of the Greens were also aware of the fact that their party was relatively weak in Lafontaine's own state of Saarland, not least because his leftist stance appealed to the post-materialist vote that they relied upon. Finally, Schröder himself and the coterie of modernisers around him were campaigning under the slogan of the 'New Centre', with its emphasis on a more centrist and managerial form of politics. On polling day, this three-way split within the party remained unresolved and held the potential to destabilise any coalition of which the SPD was a member. Moreover, the struggle between the factions within the party would impact upon the party's own bargaining position. Under the circumstances, it is not surprising that Schröder was content to wait until after the election before showing his hand.

When the results of the elections came through on 27 September, the SPD's use of such sophisticated electioneering techniques had clearly paid off. Overall, the SPD won 40.9 per cent of the party list vote, giving them 298 seats, whilst the CDU/CSU polled 35.1 per cent and received 245 seats. In addition, the minor parties did reasonably well: with the Greens polling 6.7 per cent and gaining forty-seven seats, the FDP 6.2 per cent and forty-four seats, and the PDS 5.1 per cent and thirty-five seats (including four directly-elected constituency seats in the East) (Statistiches Bundesamt, 1998). Thus, although the SPD enjoyed a reasonable majority of fifty-three seats over the CDU/CSU, in a legislature of 669 seats they fell thirty-seven seats short of the minimum-winning majority of 335 seats. However, the FDP had ruled out any possibility of entering into coalition talks with the Social Democrats and there was no real chance of the CDU negotiating with the Greens. Therefore, the SPD was presented with the numerical imperative of negotiating with either the CDU or the Greens.

Notes

1   I wish to thank staff at the SPD's campaign headquarters for the briefing that informs this passage.

7

Party programmes, coalition strategy and bargaining

Party programmes

For the first time in the history of the Federal Republic, an incumbent government had been voted out of office. Helmut Kohl, the architect of German unity and the Federal Republic's longest serving Chancellor, had once more made history. Gerhard Schröder's own reaction betrayed some surprise at the size of the swing away from the ruling coalition. It was, he said, thanks to the strategy of the 'New Centre' that the SPD had 'managed to reach out beyond the classical SPD supporters'. Despite the euphoria that had overcome the party on election night, Schröder went on to add a note of caution by observing that 'the SPD knows that we have some difficult work ahead of us' (De-news, 28 September 1998). As events were to prove, Schröder was right.

Nevertheless, the SPD had won the election and now had to strike a coalition deal with one of the other parties. The two most probable outcomes of the bargaining process were either a Grand Coalition of the SPD and CDU or a Red–Green coalition. In theory either outcome would have put the SPD in a strong position, because the party's policy programme spanned both the traditional 'bread and butter' concerns of moderate voters as well as the more post-materialist issue agenda associated with the New Left (SPD, 1998, Bündnis '90/Die Grünen, 1998, CDU/CSU, 1998; CDU, 1998). Therefore, on most of the important issues of the day the SPD could choose to find common ground with either the Greens or the CDU. Obviously there was a certain variance in emphasis between the parties, but within the central themes of relative democratic values, management of the economy and the maintenance of social welfare, all three parties were either in broad agreement or the SPD's position neatly cut across those of the other two parties. Thus, in theoretical terms at least, the SPD was the 'median party'. That the Greens found themselves within this broad consensus would have been unthinkable a decade before and demonstrated the degree to which Fischer in particular has succeeded in moderating the Greens' ideological stance. This, of course, was fortunate because all the opinion polls indicated that 95 per cent of voters regarded the task of tackling Germany's chronically high unemployment as the number one priority (*Focus*, Wahl-Spezial/1998: 44). Therefore the ability to articulate policy areas beyond the Greens' core environmental concerns was crucial to their chances of entering government.

In addition, there were areas of potential agreement between the SPD and Greens that excluded the CDU. Inevitably they where those that stressed a more post-materialist discourse, such as societal relations and group rights. This of course was consistent with the strand of New Left ideology that had partially informed the SPD's policy stance since the period of programmatic renewal in the mid 1980s. Of note was the SPD election programme's emphasis on the need for gender equality, a more liberal approach to illegal drug use, more spending on the arts and an eventual phasing out of nuclear power. At the same time, however, the SPD was much closer to the CDU in terms of its stance on foreign policy and internal security, with the programme reaffirming the Federal Republic's commitment to NATO and advocating 'fast-track' sentencing for convicted criminals. These positions contrasted sharply with the Greens' proposal to disband NATO and use the OSCE as Germany's main security forum, as well as relying less on custodial sentences for offenders. Of course, the Greens' stance on these issues was consistent with their programmatic development, but it illustrated the need for the party to moderate its post-materialist ideology in order to enter government. Because the stakes at the Federal level were so much higher than when governing individual German states, the extent to which the Greens addressed this problem would determine whether they would enter government or remain an 'outsider' party in perpetuity. If they were to share power in Bonn, any descent into the much feared 'Red–Green chaos' of the past would never be forgiven by Germany's electorate, elites or, indeed, its allies.

Coalition strategy

Given the potential risks involved in co-operating with the Greens, many in the SPD would have preferred to go into government with the CDU – including, by all accounts, Chancellor-candidate Schröder. A Grand Coalition would have constituted a centrist 'surplus majority', which as well as being less risky than a Red–Green coalition was in keeping with the politics of the 'New Centre'. It would also have served to constrain and marginalise the influence of Oskar Lafontaine, who still held ambitions to wrest the Chancellorship from his old rival. Like Schmidt in the late 1970s, Schröder would have been able to use the constraints of the coalition agreement and convention of Ministerial autonomy to build a cross-party alliance in order to offset the influence of the SPD's left wing. For Schröder and the other 'modernisers' in the party, this would have been attractive as it would have created a sympathetic coalition for the introduction of the supply-side reforms that they felt were necessary to tackle Germany's chronic unemployment problem.

There were also good reasons for arguing that the Grand Coalition option was not the most likely option. First, the only other period of Grand Coalition government in Bonn (1966–69) coincided with a period of crisis and instability for West German democracy. In many ways the coalition worked very effectively, particularly in tackling the country's first severe economic recession of the post-war period. However, the coalition was always subject to mutual suspicion, especially from both party's activists. SPD activists were unhappy with what they regarded as their party bailing out a tired and unpopular government, whilst many in the CDU/CSU rightly worried that the SPD intended eventually to take over the government from within the coalition. Moreover the political orthodoxy in the Federal Republic is that this cartel of the two catch-all parties choked off the voice of parliamentary opposition and created a political vacuum that nurtured extremism on the political left (the APO) and the far-right (the NPD). This view was shared by many in the CDU and goes some way to explain their reluctance to participate in such an arrangement. Second, the SPD was not a 'black box'. Although the party elite enjoyed considerable room for manoeuvre, internal party opinion still had to be heeded and a significant proportion of the membership preferred a Red–Green coalition in the event of an SPD victory. For the SPD's left-wing, this was a simple ideological preference, based on an affinity with the Greens and the need to avoid being outflanked by the party's Centre-Right. For more moderate members it may have been the result of a desire to avoid a Grand Coalition for the reasons noted above. But, in weighing up the relative merits of the SPD's two potential partners, it is reasonable to assume that many Social Democrats recognised a third (instrumental) reason for choosing the Greens: the avoidance of any coalition with an unnecessarily large 'surplus majority'.

In theoretical terms, such a surplus majority coalition would disadvantage the SPD in terms of both the numerical division of posts and in terms of its policy priorities. First, it would require that the spoils of office – such as Ministerial posts and more junior positions, patronage and privileged access to client groups – would have to be spread more thinly across the coalition as whole. It would be fair to assume that the CDU would expect to receive their fair share in return for participation in any Grand Coalition. For ambitious politicians and lobbyists close to the SPD, many of whom had been kept out of national office for a generation, this made the prospect of a Grand Coalition far from attractive. Second, such an outcome would also constrain the SPD's ability to shape the overall direction of the coalition's policy making. Given their pro-business orientation and claim to economic expertise, even as a 'junior' partner the CDU would probably have demanded at least the Economics Ministry as a counter-weight to the SPD's possession of the Finance Ministry. They would almost certainly have also demand the Foreign Ministry and a handful of other 'blue-chip' posts.

By contrast, a coalition with the Greens not only held out the possibility of a greater numerical share of the available portfolios but would also ensure that most, if not all, the important 'blue-chip' posts were held by the SPD, with the exception of the Foreign Ministry (which by convention goes to the junior coalition partner). But, as already noted, the convention that the Chancellor determines the overall parameters of foreign policy meant that the SPD would still have a high degree of control over this crucial area. If they chose to bargain with the Greens, the SPD would start from a stronger position than they would when dealing with the CDU. Not only were the Greens at a numerical disadvantage *vis-à-vis* the SPD, but they also had a relatively narrow range of policy priorities. Environmental policy was their main priority, not only because of the origins of the party in the ecology movements of the 1970s but also because of their experience in Niedersachsen, where they failed to secure the Environment portfolio. Trittin in particular felt this latter point most keenly, partly because of the need to make good his strategic mistake eight years earlier and also because he was likely to become the Greens' choice for Environment Minister. Thus, the Environment Ministry was the main objective of the Greens' bargaining strategy and, in order to secure this prize, they might be willing to discount a more generous share of the spoils in order to attain their core ideological objective. Therefore it came as no surprise when the SPD announced that it was entering into coalition negotiations with the Greens.

Coalition bargaining

The first round of coalition talks took place on 3 October 1997. The two parties started with procedural matters and then tackled the core issues of unemployment and the economy. In many ways these were the issues that most divided the parties and both sides were quick to warn the other that they would not give ground. For their part, the SPD hoped that the Greens would not ramp up the bargaining process by insisting on an environmental agenda that conflicted with the need to tackle unemployment, whilst the Greens were adamant that they would leave a 'visible Green 'footprint' on the coalition document' (De-news, 3 October 1998). Altogether, seven sessions were planned. Once the core issues of unemployment and the economy were tackled, the talks would move on to public finances and the planned 'Jobs Pact' between the social partners, followed by tax reform, nuclear power, foreign affairs, defence, internal security, citizenship and pensions. Finally, there would be a week of horse-trading over the allocation of Ministries and the final coalition document would be ratified by the Greens' special conference on 23 and 24 October, followed by the SPD the following day.

Throughout the bargaining process, both parties used the public domain as a means of exerting pressure on their partner's negotiating team and lowering the expectations of party activists. Schröder was keen to reassure ordinary voters that the SPD was taking a strong line with the Greens and defending the much cherished, if environmentally damaging, privileges of the German motorist. Three days after coalitions began, he gave an interview to a popular tabloid newspaper in which he publicly warned them against what he called 'automobile-phobia', in particular the proposal to raise petrol prices and impose speed limits on the country's Autobahns (Bildzeitung, 6 October 1998). This was classic Schröder populism, and harked back to his tactics in the last year of the Niedersachsen coalition. Moreover, a plan to raise petrol prices was agreed at the negotiations! The Greens appeared to take Schröder's warning in their stride and countered by making a public claim for the Justice portfolio, on the lines of the Hessen coalition. Their spokesperson Gundula Roestel suggested that the Justice Ministry's remit should be widened to include women's issues (De-news, 8 October 1998). Clearly, both parties were setting out their stalls.

Despite this outbreak of point-scoring in public and in private, the general tenor of the negotiations was good and both sides were determined to make rapid and orderly progress. Before the talks began,

Schröder declared that he did not foresee any 'unbridgeable difficulties' (De-news, 30 September 1998) and Trittin made it clear that compromises would have to be made on both sides. The need for compromise was made all the more urgent because of the unexpectedly poor state of the Federal budget they had inherited from the outgoing coalition. The Greens would fight their corner, Trittin said, but 'there won't be money for all the projects the incoming government want to tackle' (De-news, 3 October 1998). As in Niedersachsen, financial constraints added a touch of realism to the coalition negotiations and, although these constraints were real, it is perhaps not too cynical to suspect that neither party was adverse to using the issue as a means of lowering expectations among their membership prior to publication of the agreement.

After nearly three weeks of negotiations, the formal coalition agreement between the SPD and Greens was finally signed on 22 October 1997. The document still had to be ratified by the two party congresses, but both sides expressed satisfaction with the outcome of the talks. Interestingly, some degree of conflict over posts had arisen during the negotiations but it had not been of an inter-party nature, nor had it involved the Greens. In what was to become a pattern in the early days of the coalition, the division of posts highlighted the ongoing internal conflict between the traditional and modernising wings of the SPD itself. This took the form of a turf war over the remit of the Finance and Economics Ministries and, as a result, over the direction of the SPD's core economic and monetary policy. The two protagonists were Oskar Lafontaine, who was to be Finance Minister, and Schröder's choice for the Economics post, Jost Stollmann. The SPD naturally regarded both these portfolios as within their fiat and Lafontaine clearly intended to use his post of Finance Minister as a platform from which to shape coalition policy as a whole. Given the principle of Ministerial autonomy (the *Ressortsprinzip*), this was no idle threat. To achieve his aim, it was essential for Lafontaine to establish the ascendancy of his Ministry over Stollmann's and, if possible, marginalise Stollmann himself. He set about this task by insisting that responsibility for European policy, structural policy and the annual report on the economy be transferred from the Economics Ministry to his own. For his part, Stollmann was in a difficult position. Lafontaine remained the darling of the party and the most senior figure in the coalition after the Chancellor-elect. Stollmann was a moderniser whose 'Anglo-Saxon' economic instincts (he had once worked for the Boston Consulting Group) were anathema to the majority of Social Democrats and Greens alike, and the fact that he was not a member of either party left him exposed. His only hope of protecting the Economics Ministry from Lafontaine's encroachment was the intervention of Schröder on his behalf. Stollmann had been Schröder's economics advisor and had played a central role in establishing Schröder's reputation as an economic reformer. It was also clear to everyone that Lafontaine's attack on Stollmann was in many ways a coded challenge to the authority of Schröder himself. But Stollmann was to be disappointed with his erstwhile mentor. Schröder did nothing to rein in Lafontaine's empire-building activities, the Economics Ministry was stripped of its responsibilities and –one day before the coalition agreement was signed – Stollmann resigned from the Cabinet team in disgust. Schröder had avoided a confrontation with his great rival, but it was to be a decision he would soon regret.

With the Stollmann affair resolved, all parties to the agreement got to work to rally support for it and reassure their own activists in the run-up to the special party conferences. Lafontaine praised the overall agreement and stated that priority would be given to tackling the three themes of unemployment, ecological tax reform and the phasing out of nuclear energy. At the same time, he went on to stress the differences that still remained between the two parties and declared that the SPD would not allow itself to be damaged through its co-operation with the Greens (De-news, 22 October 1998). A few days later, Dieter Schulte, the chief of the German Federation of Trade unions (DGB) praised the planned Alliance for Jobs and called the overall agreement a 'step in the right direction' (De-news, 26 October 1998). At the Greens' conference, Trittin also praised the planned reform of Germany's illiberal citizenship laws and, in a sharp reference to the period of National Socialism, declared them 'a break with the logic of Blood and Land' (*TAZ*, 26 October 1998). There were, of course, critics of the agreement. Stollmann continued to criticise what he regarded as Lafontaine's domination of the new coalition and its lack of business acumen (De-news, 22 October 1998), whilst pro-business SPD figures such as Wolfgang Clement, the Minister President of Nordrhein-Westfalen, were highly critical of what they regarded as the negative impact of the planned ecological tax reforms on the economy (*Die Welt*, 27 October 1998). After much debate, both party congresses approved the coalition agreement – in the case of the SPD, almost unanimously.

In retrospect, it is no surprise that the coalition negotiations went smoothly and were ratified by both party congresses. After all, both parties were aware that this was their first, and possibly last, chance to implement a genuine reform programme at the Federal level. For the Greens in particular, whose vote in the 1998 elections had declined on that of 1994, it was by no means clear that such a chance would come again. But the relative ease with which the coalition bargaining was completed can also be explained by the division of spoils between the two parties. Take, for instance, the share of portfolios allocated to the Greens. As discussed earlier in this book, the combination of a numerical disadvantage and an ideological fixation on acquiring the Environment portfolio should have resulted in a weakened bargaining position for the Greens. It would be safe to assume that such a weakened position would have manifested itself in a reduction in both its aggregate share of portfolios and its ability to shape the policy agenda. However in practice, the actual allocation of portfolios does not reflect this. In numerical terms, the SPD share of eleven Ministerial portfolios was nearly four times higher than the three Ministries granted to the Greens. But, in terms of the ratio between parliamentary seats and portfolios, the Greens actually did almost twice as well as the SPD (Statistiches Bundesamt, SPD/*Die Grünen*, 1998) in that it took almost twenty-eight SPD parliamentary seats to 'generate' one Ministerial portfolio, whilst the Greens' ratio was only sixteen to one. This meant that in numerical terms, the Greens did proportionally better than the SPD despite the fact that the Social Democrats were in a theoretically stronger bargaining position. Still, in terms of the ideological distribution of portfolios between the parties, the SPD did much better. The Greens failed to acquire a blue-chip portfolio other than the Foreign Ministry, although they did acquire the crucial Environment Ministry and – with the creation of a separate Ministry for Health – avoid the construction of an unwieldy 'super-Ministry'. At the same time, the SPD came out of the negotiations with the Finance, Economics and Industry Ministries, as well as reserving as many as possible of those portfolios that might be deemed 'sensitive' (such as the Ministry of Justice). In addition, although the Economics Ministry was awarded to the non-partisan Werner Müller, his relatively orthodox views on the economy and his closeness to the Chancellor made his appointment effectively an SPD portfolio. All in all the SPD had held on to all the 'core' portfolios, in keeping with the established 'Red–Green model' developed at state-level.

The coalition agreement between the SPD and the Greens represents an equitable division of the spoils of office. In terms of policy making, neither party had reason to be dissatisfied with their share of the portfolios. The SPD had ensured that it had no reason to fear the Green tail wagging the Social Democratic dog, whilst the Greens' three Ministries gave them a solid platform from which to launch a raft of ecological and social reforms. For the time being at least, both parties were content. The appointment of Jürgen Trittin as Environment Minister provoked some concern amongst German producer interests, but his influence was considered to be offset by Joschka Fischer. Against the background of a healthy trade surplus, falling unemployment and analysts forecasting growth rates of around 3 per cent in 1997–98, the newly appointed Chancellor Schröder pledged his commitment to sound economic management. Everything appeared set fair for the biggest political experiment in the history of the Federal Republic.

8

Red–Green in power

Constraints on the Red–Green coalition

In the sixteen years in which the SPD were out of power in Bonn, the Federal Republic of Germany had undergone considerable socio-economic and structural change. As a result, the country they inherited following the Kohl years was in many ways a different one than the West Germany of the 1960s and 1970s. There was no going back to the trusted tenets of traditional Social Democracy. In particular, the effects of Unification had altered the parameters of state power and presented a new set of economic and political challenges. At the same time, the Federal Republic's long-established system of co-operative Federalism was regarded in some quarters as having become an obstacle to internal reform.

Although Germany's economic position remained strong, the days of the economic miracle were well and truly over. By the late 1970s, the old West Germany – like all of the advanced industrial countries – was beginning to suffer region-specific or sector-specific structural imbalances. In particular, a gap in industrial performance opened up between the automobile, machine-tool and industrial-electronics industries, primarily clustered in the southern states, and the declining steel and shipbuilding industries in the north. German policy responded to this by facilitating a shift of emphasis away from co-ordinated action between government and producer interest peak associations, such as the Federation of German Industry (the BDI) or the Federation of German Employers (the BDA). As a result, the co-ordinating role of sectoral organisations, such as the Chemical Industry Association (the VCI), and the Chemical Industry Employers Association (the BVAC) grew in importance. The emphasis of policy making shifted from a 'national' frame towards regional- or sector-specific issues. Emphasis was placed upon successful or unsuccessful regions (Bayern or Bremen) and sectors (automobiles or shipbuilding). Throughout the 1980s, imbalances grew between north and south, and the so-called 'sun-rise' and 'rust-belt' industries. These imbalances had a political dimension, in that the northern states (such as Gerhard Schröder's Niedersachsen) tended to be SPD-run while the Christian Democrats were stronger in the south. This inevitably had an impact on the priorities set by the CDU/CSU–FDP administration in Bonn. During the 1980s, the focus of policy moved towards the meso-level and away from the model of nationally co-ordinated 'concerted action' associated with, for example, the Brandt era. There were *ad hoc* national agreements in the period following unification, such as the 'Solidarity Pact' of 1992. But any attempt by the incoming government to permanently revive the patterns of macro-corporatism prevalent in the 1970s would have been bucking the established trend of the previous two decades. The SPD had to work within the more limited scope of state intervention that they inherited from the outgoing government.

Unification involved the accession into the Federal Republic of five new states whose structural problems made those facing the northern states pale into insignificance. Indeed the immediate effect of unification was such that in the early 1990s the disparity between Western Germany and five new states widened. Stimulated by demand from both the new states and Central and Eastern Europe, the West boomed, with growth rates of over 3 per cent per annum between 1990 and 1993. At the same time, the shake-out of inefficient industrial production in the East led to a decline in overall growth of about 10 per cent year-on-year over the same period. When this initial spurt of growth in the West came to an end, the Federal Republic's economy stagnated and unemployment rose steadily over the decade to over four million, or 10 per cent of the workforce. Clearly, urgent reforms were needed in order to tackle the Federal Republic's structural imbalances and growing army of unemployed. Doubts had been voiced about the ability of Germany to respond effectively to these challenges (Katzenstein, 1987: 35). It is argued that there were three main reasons for this. First, the structure and norms of the administrative apparatus. Second, the 'segmentation' or 'sectorisation' (Bulmer, 1983: 350) of German public policy through the system of co-operative federalism, and the party system's tendency to produce coalition governments. Third, the diverse public and private interests that are able to influence the policy debate (Katzenstein, 1987: 35–60) and serve as veto points on political innovation.

The post-1945 settlement established the principle of political parties being central to the governmental/administrative nexus of the new Federal Republic. At the same time, the administrative culture within the permanent civil service remained deeply rationalistic and expert oriented. As a result, the Federal Republic is torn between two competing ethoses: that of the modern 'party state' (*Parteienstaat*) and the residual Prussian ideal of the 'administrator state' (*Beamtenstaat*). This interdependence of the established parties and the administrative structures led to a high degree of partisan penetration of the civil service. For instance, in 1972 over half the senior posts (state secretaries, heads and departmental heads of division) at the state and federal level of the civil service were such appointments. It also had a profound effect on the parties themselves, particularly in discursive terms, with administrative values permeating internal debate within the established parties (Lees, 1995: 9) and reinforcing the existing consensus between them on the substantive issues of state. The net result of this, of course, was to privilege path-dependent policy options over more innovative solutions, serving as a constraint upon the kind of political innovation seen elsewhere.

Germany's federal structure added further constraints, through the division of competencies between the Federation and the states. During the 1980s and 1990s, the states not only managed to defend a great deal of their constitutional powers, but actually won new ones. For instance, during the Single European Act and Maastricht Treaty ratification processes, the Federation was forced to cede a right of co-decision (*Mitwirkung*) to the states and enhanced the role of the Bundesrat in the formulation and scrutiny of European legislation (Paterson, 1996: 178. see also Jeffery, 1994.). But even before these changes were made, the states enjoyed considerable influence over policy making and, quite often, this influence was used for party political purposes. Individual states also have their own particular policy priorities and, as a result, even states governed by the same party often came into conflict with the Federal government. For instance, in the mid 1990s Kurt Biedenkopf (the CDU Minister President of Saxony) defied the Kohl government and refused to withdraw financial sweeteners to VW to locate in his state, despite it being ruled against by European Union competition law.

The party system appeared to further constrain the ability of any government to respond effectively to the Federal Republic's systemic problems, because of the tendency towards coalition government and the strength of the principle of Ministerial autonomy (Article 65 of the Basic Law – the *Ressortsprinzip*). The distribution of Ministerial seats is central to the political balance of any coalition and, given the tendency of parties to staff Ministries with their own people, policy making can become an adjunct to inter-coalition rivalry. 'Junior' partners within coalitions – such as the FDP or Greens – regard the principle of Ministerial autonomy as a valuable restraint on their more powerful partner and a safeguard of their own interests. As a result, they defend their Ministerial 'turf' jealously, leading to differences in policy style and content across competing Ministries (see Paterson, 1989: 73–89, Weidner, 1995: 13–14).

Finally, political innovation is further constrained by the large number of parapublic institutions – such as producer groups' peak associations, citizens' initiative groups and NGOs – that have over the years acquired a high degree of purchase on the policy process in the Federal Republic. The impact of these parapublic institutions has less to do with inputs (unsolicited policy initiatives) than with their ability to shape outputs through legal redress, etc. (Kitschelt, 1986, Paterson, 1989, Lees, 1995). As Bodo Hombach observed around the time of the Bundestag elections, this ability to shape outputs means that narrow sectional interests have the ability to impose what is effectively a veto on initiatives that they perceive to be against their interests.

Taken together, these three sets of structural constraints impose limits on what is politically possible in the Federal Republic. But it does not necessarily follow that system performance is eroded as result. As Goldberger points out, Germany's decentralised policy-making apparatus 'makes unified policy making and co-ordination more difficult than in its more unitary neighbours' (1993: 291). At the same time, it can be argued that where 'detailed tasks require a uniform and agreed co-operation of all the participants' (Kunze, 1968, cited Bulmer and Paterson, 1987: 187), the system facilitates consensual policy formulation. Nevertheless, the emphasis upon consensus means that the German policy apparatus can be, or at least appear to be, slow to respond effectively to new problems. Katzenstein asserts that 'major changes in policy stand little chance of success' (1987: 35) under present conditions. In truth, Germany's record is more mixed than any of the above comments indicate. On the one hand, the Federal Republic's record in areas such as environmental policy is good compared with some other European states. On the other, aspects of the Federal Republic's regulatory framework appear to many Anglo-Saxon observers as verging on the antediluvian. What the structures of German governance do not facilitate, is the kind of non-consensual, innovative political agendas associated with the Thatcher or Blair governments in Great Britain. And for Gerhard Schröder, who came to power portraying himself as a moderniser in the Blair mould, this was to prove a significant problem.

Policy priorities

Whichever party had won the 1998 Bundestag elections would have been confronted with four interrelated political dillemas. These were, first, the need to tackle unemployment, second, to enhance Germany's attractiveness as a place of investment (the so-called *Standort* problem), third, to tackle the 'reform blockage' (*Reformstau*) within the Federal Republic's political and policy-making apparatus and, fourth, to counter an increasing popular mood of disenchantment with the political process (*Politikverdrossenheit*) – especially in the East.

The new Red–Green coalition identified three main themes which they hoped would provide the core of their programme. First, the reduction of unemployment by a million over the four-year term. Second, withdrawal from the use of nuclear power and a parallel programme of ecological tax reform. Third, the reform of Germany's outdated citizenship laws, in order better to reflect the multi-cultural reality of contemporary life in the Federal Republic. These were all worthy political objectives, but only one of them could be regarded as a traditional social democratic concern. The other two were the result of 'New Left' thinking within the party and, of course, co-operation with the Greens. As a result, the new coalition was also committed to an additional raft of policies, some of which distracted from the resolution of the four core issues, or even conflicted with them.

Economic and fiscal reform

Both parties made it clear that tackling unemployment and the 'Standort' problem was the highest priority. When he took over as Federal Chancellor, Gerhard Schröder re-emphasised his claim that his term in office should be judged by the government's ability to tackle Germany's chronically high rate of unemployment. This was around 10.5 per cent in the Autumn of 1998, but was to rise sharply thereafter – reaching 11.5 per cent by the second month of 1999 (up 250,000 in January alone). With unemployment rising at such a rate – and with so much political capital invested in bringing it down – the new government opted for a mix of measures. Some of these were short-term initiatives, designed as much to reassure their supporters as to make a lasting impact, whilst others were more long term in nature. Of these long-term measures, some relied on long-established corporatist practice, whilst others were supply-side measures designed to boost efficiency. At the same time, the coalition introduced other legislation that appeared to undermine the very effi-ciency gains they were trying to make.

The most notable short-term measure was an emergency programme to tackle youth unemployment. To do this, the government intended to co-opt the Federal Labour Agency's current account rather than wait for funds to be made available in due course. Compared with other Western European countries such as France, the Federal Republic did not have a particularly bad youth unemployment problem. But it was high in his-torical terms and regarded as a top priority. As Trittin declared at the start of the coalition negotiations, 'we will rip into employing and training 100,000 young persons straight away, and we will not make it dependent upon the 'Alliance for Jobs'. It is an emergency measure we will not com-promise upon' (De-news, 3 October 1998).

Nevertheless, it was the Alliance for Jobs that was intended to provide the core of the new government's policy to tackle unemployment. It was intended that the Alliance for Jobs was to be more than an *ad hoc* forum of the social partners and would have a formal institutional structure and a clear set of operational parameters. Structurally, the Alliance was to be divided into two tiers. In the first tier there were to be three 'broad-brush' working groups. The first was a rolling set of 'summit talks' (*Spitzenge-spräch*) between the producers' peak associations (the BDI, BDA, the Chambers of Commerce, the DGB, DAG and various trade unions) and the government (the Chancellor, the Minister for the Chancellor's Office and the Finance, Economics, Labour and Health Ministries).[1] Working next to the summit group was a steering committee (*Steurungsgruppe*) tasked with the co-ordination and approval of a set of working groups (see below) and the preparation of documentation for the summit talks. This group was led by the Minister for the Chancellor's Office, Bodo Hombach. Hombach also chaired the third 'benchmarking group', com-prising practitioners and academics, which was tasked with the job of comparing Germany's economic and social policy with internationally recognised best practice. The second tier of the Alliance was made up of a number of working and expert groups (*Arbeits- und Expertgruppen*), including representatives from the government, industry and the trade unions. These would tackle themes such as education and training, life-long learning and reform of health provision. The operational parame-ters were clearly set out. There was to be a deliberate move away from what were regarded as failed solutions such as work creation programmes and early retirement, as well as a questioning of statist solutions and an acceptance of the need to develop the service sector of the economy.

Superficially at least, this 'cartel against unemployment' (Der Spiegel, 10 May 1999) appeared to be a serious effort to break with the past. Many of the ideas underlying the Alliance – such as benchmarking and the promotion of service provision – indicated a willingness to look beyond the settled practice of the Federal Republic and find innovative solutions to Germany's structural unemployment problem. But the corporatist structures employed to do this remained as path-dependent as ever and were to prove the weak link in the Alliance for Jobs concept. It was interesting that such a self-proclaimed moderniser as Schröder should put his faith in an old-fashioned corporatist solution in order to tackle the problem. This obvious conflict between self-perception and practice was typical of Schröder's political style and would become an issue in itself within the year. The pact is the type of arrangement that plays to Schröder's strengths, allowing him to take on the role of facilitator between business and organised labour and hammer out a plan of action with the social partners. But such arrangements rely on compromise rather than innovation and tend to generate path-dependent policy initiatives. The template for the Alliance for Jobs was the period of 'concerted action' (*Konzertierte Aktion*) in the late 1960s and early 1970s. Concerted action provided a stable corporatist framework within which the social partners addressed the economic problems associated with the end of the economic miracle, the collapse of Bretton Woods, and the subsequent oil shocks of the 1970s. It would be much more difficult to replicate such an institution in the very different social and economic conditions of the late 1990s and, to date, the Alliance for Jobs has not delivered the changes in practices and subsequent reduction in unemployment that was hoped for.

Alongside the corporatism of the Alliance for Jobs, the new government also planned a raft of supply-side measures more associated with a modernising agenda. A wholesale reform of the Federal Republic's tax system was proposed, with the aim of simplifying the system, squeezing out tax loopholes and reducing the burden of non-wage labour costs that were discouraging employers from taking on more labour. An attempt was also to be made to tackle the country's unsustainable pensions system, as well as the increasingly expensive system of health insurance. However, the increased contributions and cuts in pension provision planned by the outgoing coalition were reversed and emphasis placed upon changes such as separate provision for dependent women and the encouragement of more private provision. It was hoped that health spending would be capped through yearly global budgeting and a renewed emphasis on the family GP as the first stop and gatekeeper of health care provision (SPD/Die Grunen, 1998).

The problem with these proposed reforms was that none of them really got to grips with the deep-seated structural problems that the Federal Republic faced. In this, the new government was no worse than the out-going Kohl administration which had repeatedly ducked the issue since taking power in the early 1980s. Moreover, the necessities of political campaigning had led the SPD to commit itself to reversing those limited, but unpopular, reforms (such as on pension provision) that had been planned. This was the inevitable consequence of representative politics.

Nevertheless, the weakness of the new coalition's economic policies went deeper than this. Some reforms, such as the proposal to regulate and extend social protection to the Federal Republic's small part-time sector – the so-called '620 Mark jobs' – enhanced social justice and were consistent with Social Democratic ideology. However, in increasing the level of non-wage labour costs in this sector, they were not consistent with the desire to generate employment growth. Other proposed reforms, in the short term at least, seemed in direct contradiction to the goal of freeing-up the economy and stimulating job creation. Now ensconced in his enhanced Finance Ministry, Oskar Lafontaine's plan to reform the Federal Republic's tax system included a proposal to introduce a set of so-called 'eco-taxes', using the 'polluter pays' principle. The purpose of the eco-tax was to shift the burden of taxation towards consumption, through an increase in duty on fuel and energy and a reform of Germany's system of corporate taxation. Over time such a reform would be expected to enhance employment growth, because the price of labour compared to other factor costs would decline in relative terms. This would in turn lower the marginal cost of each new unit of labour and – all things being equal – make it more attractive for employers to take on additional work-ers. In the short term, however, such a reform had the potential to be politically very costly indeed. The new eco-taxes would affect businesses and individuals alike and, while the benefits of such reforms would be slow to become apparent, the costs would be immediately obvious. For example, Lafontaine intended to raise the duty paid on petrol by 6 pfen-nigs a year until 2003 and, in a country where the motorist is king, such a move was not going to be universally popular! Experience at the state level – such as the imposition of a speed limit on Berlin's AVUS motorway in 1989 – suggested that this was a politically risky course to take, whilst any-thing that appeared to add to the burden on industry would mobilise pro-ducer interests against the new government.

Some of the criticism of the proposed eco-tax came from predictable quarters. For instance, the head of the BDI, Olaf Henkel, called the package a threat to the labour market (Handelsblatt, 13 October 1998), whilst the President of the BDA, Dieter Hundt, referred to it as a 'deterrence programme' against investors (De-news, 22 October 1998). More worryingly for the government, criticism also came from within the SPD – particularly from those considered to be close to Schröder. Schröder's disgruntled former economics advisor, Jost Stollmann, continued his offensive against what he saw as evidence of Lafontaine's dominance of the new government. It was, he said, a setback for the entire 'New Centre' project (*Süddeutsche Zeitung*, 22 October 1998). Wolfgang Clement, the Minister President of North Rhine Westphalia, went as far as to criticise the eco-tax plans at the SPD's special conference to ratify the coalition agreement (De-news, 27 October 1998). With the new coalition still basking in the glow of their election victory, such critical voices were in a minority. But this was soon to change. Despite overseeing a Red–Green coalition in his own state, Clement's instincts were those of a pro-business moderniser and, as such, he was someone whom Schröder needed to keep on board. But Clement – like other SPD reformers – was disturbed by what he regarded as the anti-business tone of many of the coalition's policies and was wary of Lafontaine's apparent dominance of its agenda.

Trittin and nuclear policy

Clement's interventions were not to be limited to criticising Lafontaine's policies. Soon he would become embroiled in the row over the coalitions plans to phase out nuclear power. As discussed earlier in the book, the Greens' core concern was environmental policy and possession of the Environment portfolio was effectively non-negotiable. If tackling unemployment was the primary concern of the government as a whole, for many Greens the phasing out of nuclear energy was their main goal and, with Jürgen Trittin in charge of the Environment Ministry, they had high hopes of progress on this front. But, within months of coming to power, Trittin and his supporters' hopes were to be frustrated.

Trittin's planned withdrawal from the use of nuclear power entailed two steps. First, he intended to revise the Federal energy law and establish a legal framework for withdrawal from nuclear power. Second, the revised law would then provide a basis for so-called 'consensus talks' with the nuclear industry in order to hammer out a timetable for such a process. On the surface this seemed a practical proposal, and was similar in structure to the talks on nuclear energy that took place in Niedersachsen during the 1990–94 coalition. But such talks take time and Trittin required a quick victory in order to placate the more vociferous antinuclear campaigners within his party's ranks. Therefore, Trittin proposed that the Federal Republic should move quickly to end the re-processing of nuclear fuel. This proposed unilateral action was to prove a step too far. It provided Trittin's opponents with a single issue around which to to mobilise in order to water down the whole package.

The suggestion that the Federal Republic unilaterally cancel its contracts with re-processing plants in France and Britain generated a low-level intergovernmental row with European neighbours on the eve of the Federal Republic's term holding the Presidency of the European Union. British Nuclear Fuels then threatened to respond to what would have been a major blow to the British re-processing industry by returning unprocessed fuel rods to the Federal Republic. Memories of the civil disobedience associated with the transportation of nuclear waste to dumps such as Gorleben were still fresh in many state politicians' minds, and this provoked a harsh response from both Clement and Gerhard Glogowski, the Minister President of Niedersachsen at the time (and another close associate of Schröder). The two main long-term nuclear storage facilities in the Federal Republic were sited in Nordrhein-Westfalen and Niedersachsen and the two states would be delegated to handle the security for such transports – with all the financial and political costs that this would entail.

By the beginning of 1999, Trittin's impatience had ranged a formidable set of political opponents against him – both domestic and international, from the private sector and from within the coalition itself. These pressures might still have been resisted if Trittin had the support of Schröder. But Schröder had no intention of supporting Trittin on this issue. He had no great enthusiasm for closing down the nuclear power industry and was anxious not to annoy other European governments. Moreover, although they had worked together in Niedersachsen, Schröder and Trittin did not get along particularly well and the Chancellor was obviously more comfortable doing business with Fischer rather than Trittin. However, Schröder also gave the impression that the force of special interest pleading had persuaded him to backtrack on what was a clear pledge in the coalition agreement, signed just months before. Throughout the winter of 1998–99 the nuclear industry, supported by German industrialists terrified of higher energy costs, kept up a steady PR offensive against Trittin's proposals. For instance, the the chief of the power-generating company *Viag*, Wilhelm Simson, described them as 'totally unacceptable' (*Der Spiegel*, 25 January 1999: 26). At the heart of this campaign was the 'Standort' issue – that Germany had become an unattractive location for investment and that nothing must be done to make this position worse.

The 'Standort' argument was a powerful one, even if it sometimes flew in the face of the facts. As described earlier, Schröder had given short shrift to the proposal, put forward during the coalition negotiations, to impose a speed limit on Germany's autobahns. Obviously, this was partly out of fear of antagonising ordinary motorists who regarded the freedom to drive as fast as their vehicle would permit as being an inalienable right. But it was also the result of concerted lobbying by the motor industry itself. The Chairmen of Volkswagen and BMW had publicly condemned the proposals, calling them an economic disaster that would only serve to generate jobs in Italy, France and South Korea (De-news, 13 October 1998). Why the imposition of a speed limit would drive jobs away from Germany – but create them in competitor countries that already had such limits on their own roads – was never made clear. Playing the 'Standort' card exposed politicians who supported the proposals to the allegation that they were damaging German competitiveness. The political damage had been done and the idea of a national speed limit was quietly shelved.

Of course, the question of phasing out nuclear power was a more difficult one. The issues were more complex and there was little to be learned from experiences elsewhere. On the one hand, the 'Standort' argument – that phasing out nuclear power would costs jobs in the industry itself and increase energy costs for German manufacturers – was a powerful one. In addition, the environmental argument was not conclusive either and there was some truth in the argument that in the short term the phasing out of nuclear power would make the economy more reliant on fossil fuels and increase emissions of greenhouse gasses. On the other hand, the Federal Republic already had one of the most effective environmental regimes in the world and there was evidence that this had, if anything, enhanced the economy's competitiveness (Weale, 1992). The more effective enforcement of existing legislation (*nach Gesetz und Recht*) and the introduction of tighter controls on emissions and the disposal of waste had stimulated innovation and, over time, helped raise productivity levels in those industries effected. It had also created the conditions for the growth of a new generation of small-to-medium sized companies – developing new power technologies such as wind power and solar power – who were years ahead of their equivalents in countries with more lax regimes, such as the United Kingdom. But opinion was divided over the issue. Even the President of the Institute for Climate, Environment and Energy argued that it was not realistic to expect a complete shut-down of nuclear reactors in less than thirty years (De-news, 20 October 1998).

Given the complexity of the issue and the political and economic stakes involved, any attempt to negotiate a relatively quick withdrawal from nuclear power would require the kind of tact and political antenna that Trittin did not possess. By pushing too hard too early on the issue he not only antagonised the interests with which he had to strike a deal, but he also gave Schröder the perfect opportunity to assert his authority over the coalition and re-affirm his pro-business credentials. Trittin had walked into a trap of his own making and Schröder forced his Environment Minister to climb down in public. Trittin's plan to set an overall deadline for withdrawal was parked and it was decided that the future shut-down of any of the Federal Republic's nineteen nuclear reactors would be decided on the merits of each case. In the short term at least, Trittin's programme was on hold and the initiative was back with the nuclear industry. The Greens' were outraged as this setback and some parliamentarians called for the party to leave the coalition immediately. Others, such as Fischer, took a more cautious stance on the issue. They too were disappointed at the failure of the Greens to achieve what many regarded as their main goal in government, but they also recognised the complexity of the issues involved – not least the element of scientific doubt that existed and the interdependence of German nuclear industry with the rest of Europe. Many of them also placed the blame on Trittin himself for over-reaching himself, and his authority within the party was diminished as a result.

Reform of the citizenship laws

The nuclear issue was a complex one, cross-cutting the environmental and 'Standort' debates, in which both sides were able to harness scientific opinion in their support. It was perhaps no surprise, therefore, that it would prove difficult to resolve. However, the third plank in the new coalition's programme – the reform of Germany's citizenship laws – appeared on the surface to be fairly straightforward debate between two competing ideas of citizenship. The existing citizenship law, based on the 'Reichs- und Staatsangehrigkeits Gesetz' (*RuStAG*) of 1913, was firmly grounded within the idea of an ethnic or blood-related concept of citizenship ('Ius Sanguinis'). In theory and, sometimes, in practice, the logical conclusion of such a law was to privilege 'ethnic Germans'

(*Volksdeutsche*) from Eastern Europe over second or third generation descendants of immigrants from southern Europe. Yet the Federal Republic had undergone huge socio-economic change in the post-war period, not least because of its relative economic success. The economic miracle of the 1950s tightened the indigenous labour market and generated a demand for cheap labour from countries such as Italy, Turkey and Yugoslavia. It was intended that the immigrants who came to Germany under the 'Guest Worker' (*Gastarbeiter*) system would leave again after a number of years but, inevitably, many settled in the Federal Republic. Nevertheless, the popular discourse of 'German' identity remained one of a shared ethnicity and cultural homogeneity. This was increasingly at odds with what was, in the major cities at least, a multi-cultural society. It was clear to many Germans that the citizenship law had become inappropriate to the social conditions of Germany today.

Within the new coalition, reform of the Federal Republic's citizenship law in principle was not a contested idea. But there were profound differences of opinion about their proposed scope. As Trittin's declaration at his party conference demonstrated, the Greens were overwhelmingly in favour of the reforms. On the other hand, some within the SPD were more cautious about them and feared a backlash from their core blue-collar electorate. Interior Minister Otto Schilly – ironically an ex-Green – had publicly stated that immigration into Germany had reached a point where any further increase would damage the fabric of the Republic. This had provoked an angry reaction from the Greens. Fischer called the whole debate 'ill-advised' whilst Daniel Cohn-Bendit – the veteran of Paris 1968 and now an MEP – accused Schilly of 'talking without thinking' (*TAZ*, 22 October 1998). Press opinion was more divided on the issue. One the one hand, the respected weekly newspaper *Die Zeit* unequivocally stated that Schilly was 'wrong' whilst, on the other, the left-leaning *Der Spiegel*'s coverage of the issue was more ambivalent. It reported the internal coalition debate in quite a neutral manner but also saw fit to run a story about foreigners, drugs and violent crime in Berlin's Wedding district in the same feature (*Der Spiegel*, 23 October 1998)! What was clear was that Schilly had tapped into a popular sentiment, with opinion polls indicating that over half of the population believed that there were 'too many' foreigners in the Federal Republic (Emnid. in ibid.). Nevertheless, Red–Green coalitions at the state level had always pushed for the extension of rights to immigrants, such as the right to vote in state elections. Up until now, the existing Federal law had severely limited their scope for extending rights to foreigners. Now that there was a

Red–Green coalition in power at the Federal level, it was expected that they would move quickly to amend the law.

Up until early February 1999, the coalition's plans to reform the Federal Republic's citizenship laws appeared to be on course. The CDU/CSU had launched a signature campaign against it but this appeared to many to be more an exercise in populism than a serious attempt to stop the reforms. The extent to which the Christian Democrats were tapping into the fears of 'ordinary' Germans was not fully appreciated until the defeat of the ruling Red–Green coalition in state elections in Hessen in early February 1999. The CDU's effective use of the race card led to an increase in their vote of around 4 per cent, whilst the Greens – who regarded Hessen as one of their strongholds – saw their vote halved. The SPD's vote increased, but by less than 2 per cent, which indicated that they had not picked up the votes lost by their coalition partners. The CDU had obviously struck a political nerve.

The Hessen result spelt the end of the new citizenship law in its original form, although a revised law was eventually passed by the German parliament. It was also a serious blow to the future of the Red–Green coalition itself. The loss of the SPD's majority in the Bundesrat meant that the coalition had to deal with the same institutional gridlock that dogged the last years of Helmut Kohl's government. The SPD was to go on to suffer a series of setbacks in state elections in, for example, Berlin and Bremen which would eventually threaten the coalition and Schröder's position as Chancellor. But the Hessen result was the first tangible evidence of growing disillusionment with the Red–Green coalition. Revitalised by the campaign against the citizenship law, the CDU/CSU now held the balance of power. The government had to compromise with them in order to ensure the passage of legislation through the second chamber. Ironically, Schröder now found himself in what many regarded as a *de facto* Grand Coalition after all.

Lafontaine the 'loose cannon'

But worse was yet to come. Ever since Schröder beat Lafontaine to the nomination for Chancellor-candidate, an uneasy peace had existed between the two men. In the run-up to the Bundestag elections this peace had held, given the need to show a united front and deny the CDU/CSU the opportunity to capitalise on any evidence of internal strife within the SPD. Nevertheless, no-one assumed that Lafontaine had given up his ambition to become Chancellor and his ruthlessly effective management of the period of coalition bargaining had left him in a very powerful position indeed. The new Federal Finance Minister had effectively marginalised the Economics Ministry and, with it, what should have been the institutional and ideological counter-weight to Lafontaine in the Cabinet. Lafontaine also retained his post of Chairperson of the SPD, and had further consolidated his position by forcing Rudolf Scharping to resign as leader of the SPD's parliamentary faction. Fearing an open row during the coalition negotiations, Schröder brokered a deal between the two men – with Scharping being offered the post of Defence Minister as compensation. But with Scharping at Defence, and Stollmann having refused the truncated Economics Ministry, the only economic modernisers of any weight left in the Cabinet were Bodo Hombach and Schröder himself. As Minister for the Cabinet Office, Hombach had Schröder's confidence but lacked the power-base and political skills to counter the influence of Lafontaine. As for the Chancellor, he seemed unwilling or unable to rein in his Finance Minister – much to the alarm of Schröder's allies in the party. The most vocal of these was Clement, whose opposition to Lafontaine's tax proposals remained implacable. In an interview with the magazine *Focus*, Clement called on the coalition to make a radical change in direction. Lafontaine's plans, he said, were a burden on the economy and he called for a drastic cut in income tax and repeal of the regulation of the low-pay '620 Mark' sector (De-news, 24 November 1998). But Lafontaine, a convinced Keynesian, was determined to push ahead with his tax reforms. Although the overall package was revenue-neutral, it did widen the tax base and target limited cuts on the low-paid. This fiscal package was 'Keynesian demand stimulus, Lafontaine style' (*The European*, 19–25 October 1998: 9) and he clearly wanted it to be complemented by a loosening of monetary policy. To this end Lafontaine publicly called on the Bundesbank to cut its interest rates, in a clear challenge to its coveted independence. He had become something of a 'loose cannon'.

Lafontaine's ambitions were not confined to Germany alone. By the start of 1999, Social Democrat-led governments were in power in the majority of European Union member states. These included the three most important EU countries, Germany, France and the United Kingdom. However there were distinct differences in the nature of 'social democracy' in the three states, not least between the 'traditional' social democracy of the Jospin government in France and the more neo-liberal approach of Blair's 'New Labour' government in the UK. Jospin's PS took a more interventionist approach to state public policy and saw the EU as a potential bulwark against what the French regarded as the less attractive aspects of globalisation. Blair, by contrast, was pro-business and regarded globalisation as more of an opportunity than a threat. He also had ambitions to shape the EU agenda, by making it a more open economy that would adapt to the challenges of the global market.

If the positions of France and the UK appeared to be polar opposites, the Federal Republic gave the impression of maintaining an equidistance between them. But the position was more complex than that. In reality the ideological struggle between the two paradigms of social democracy actually cross-cut the SPD – with Lafontaine firmly in the 'French' camp and Schröder appearing to lean more towards the 'Blairite' model (Lees, 2000). The personal struggle for power between the two men had always been over-written by an ideological divide (although it was never clear if Schröder adopted the mantle of moderniser out of conviction or for tactical and opportunistic reasons). With the new government busy forging links with the governments of its EU neighbours, this struggle was projected on to the business of statecraft itself.

Given Lafontaine's ideological certainty – and Schröder's more pragmatic approach – it is no surprise that it was Lafontaine who adopted the higher profile in the early months of the coalition. There were two reasons for this. First the Federal Republic traditionally regarded France, rather than the UK, as its most important ally in Europe. Although its influence is sometimes over-stated, the Franco-German alliance had acted as the motor of European integration since the creation of the European Coal and Steel Community in the early 1950s. More recently, Helmut Kohl and Francois Mitterand were at the forefront of the Single Market programme and the Treaty on European Union. Lafontaine's views on European policy were close to those of French Finance Minister Dominique Strauss-Kahn and the two politicians soon struck up a strategic alliance to further their common goals.

The second reason for Lafontaine's ascendancy over Schröder in these early months was timing. The last months of 1998 were dominated by two issues – the economic crisis in Asia and the run-up to the launch of the Euro in January 1999. For interventionists like Lafontaine and Strauss-Kahn the issues were linked. The crisis in Asia was evidence that the unfettered flow of capital around the globe had to be stopped, and the European Union should be used as a platform to push for such regulations. At the G7, International Monetary Fund and World Bank meetings in Washington in early October, Strauss-Kahn had proposed a 'new Bretton Woods' agreement, with managed bands for the world's major currencies. This idea was enthusiastically backed by Lafontaine. One of these major currencies was undoubtedly the new Euro itself and Lafontaine was determined to shape the policy making and, if possible, the institutional design of the new currency arrangement. At the top of his list was a re-writing of the growth and stability pact, which placed the idea of financial stability at the heart of remit of the new European Central Bank (ECB). In many ways, the ECB was modelled on the Bundesbank and the commitment to financial orthodoxy had been the *quid pro quo* for Germany giving up the Mark. Lafontaine regarded tackling unemployment in Europe as being the number one priority and, as a Keynesian, saw the ability to run deficits as being an important weapon in this battle. With the ECB locked into a monetarist model, the possibilities for macro-economic stimulus were limited. Indeed any fiscal loosening by the member states would be self-defeating, given that the ECB would have raised interest rates to off-set it, in much the same way that the Bundesbank had done to counter the effects of unification in the early 1990s. As his suggestion that they lower interest rates indicated, Lafontaine was no great admirer of the Bundesbank. Indeed, as a died-in-the-wool Social Democrat, he would have remembered how the Bundesbank had undermined the former SPD Finance Minister Karl Schiller's short-lived experiment with Keynesianism in the early 1970s. For Lafontaine, the Euro start-up was the chance to break out of the Federal Republic's monetary straightjacket. The three objectives of currency regulation at the international level, a less orthodox monetary framework within the European Union and fiscal loosening within the Federal Republic were central to his vision of how he wanted Germany and Europe to develop in the future.

Despite Lafontaine's high profile, Schröder was also undertaking his own initiatives. In November 1998, Schröder visited Tony Blair in London and the two leaders announced the setting-up of a standing committee to tackle the question of reconciling the needs of economic efficiency and social justice. It was to be jointly chaired by British Trade and Industry Secretary of the time, Peter Mandelson, and the then-Minister for the Chancellor's Office Bodo Hombach. Schröder emphasised that monetary politics must contribute to the reduction of unemployment and that this new committee would be tasked with finding some of the answers. Schröder then went on to Birmingham and gave a speech to the Confederation of British Industry. In his speech, Schröder argued that the world economy needed 'a new framework that guides the behaviour of private participants, corporations, and banks down the right paths' (De-news, 3 November 1998). At the same time, he argued that

Europe had to tackle the problems of unemployment through supply-side measures – such as increasing labour market flexibility and encouraging innovation – rather than through the demand-side policies advocated by Lafontaine.

Schröder's co-option of the British, and Lafontaine's identification with the French, meant that what was basically a struggle for power within the SPD had taken on an intergovernmental dimension. Blair and Jospin saw themselves as the potential leaders of European social democracy and both were keenly aware of the importance of the Federal Republic in this respect. Given its size, political weight and economic importance, and its ideological position between these two poles, Germany would play a pivotal role in determining the outcome of this low-key ideological tussle. It appeared the stage was set for a struggle between personalities and ideologies, which had the potential to spill over into the business of statecraft itself. It was a fascinating prospect. However, two events, one minor and one calamitous, were to change everything.

Show-down between Schröder and Lafontaine

On 11 March 1999, Oskar Lafontaine surprised everyone and announced his resignation as Finance Minister. He stepped down as Party Chairman at the same time. True to form, the charismatic left-winger departed from politics in the most high profile manner possible. Throughout the German political class, the shock of Lafontaine's resignation was palpable. Yet in retrospect it was clear that a showdown between Schröder and Lafontaine had been inevitable. For some time, Schröder had become increasingly anxious about the actions of his Finance Minister. Lafontaine's relentless empire-building had become a threat to the Chancellor's authority. Schröder had also come under a great deal of pressure from his allies both inside and outside the coalition to stop Lafontaine, who had also annoyed many of his colleagues by arguing for closer co-operation with the PDS.

Lafontaine had also over-played his hand in his Ministerial role. His public pronouncements on the need to regulate capitalism had alarmed and alienated a number of powerful constituencies at home and abroad – including industry and commerce, the ECB, many of Germany's European neighbours (including the UK) and the British tabloid press. For instance, Lafontaine had suggested that tax-harmonisation in Europe should be the next stage in the integration process. This had undermined efforts in Britain to shift public opinion on the Euro and had led to the tabloid newspaper *The Sun* to run a headline portraying Lafontaine as 'the most dangerous man in Europe'! Lafontaine's tendency to think aloud and damn the consequences was becoming increasingly counter-productive, reaching a low-point in late February and early March when he called on the ECB to cut interest rates to stimulate growth. (Lafontaine then travelled to the ECB's monthly meeting in Frankfurt to lobby ECB-chief Wim Duisenberg and his colleagues personally.) With the newly launched Euro still struggling for credibility in the markets, this was an unwelcome intervention and Duisenberg pointedly ignored Lafontaine's advice. The Federal Finance Minister had overstepped the mark and allowed himself to be humiliated.

By the beginning of March 1999, the Red–Green coalition was in seri-ous trouble. The Hessen elections the month before had knocked the government off course. Unemployment was rising rapidly and many of the coalition's policies – such as Trittin's nuclear policy and Lafontaine's tax measures – were deeply unpopular. In addition, Lafontaine's increas-ingly rash statements about the ECB were undermining the Federal Republic's tenure of the EU Council Presidency. Moreover, the system of coalition management had broken down completely. Ministers appeared to spend more time briefing against one another than standing collec-tively behind the coalition's record, whilst a series of high profile inter-ventions from the ranks of the two parties served to further undermine the authority of the government. Alarmingly for Schröder, his own approval rating began to slip. During the first months of the coalition, the Chancellor remained far more popular than the coalition itself and enjoyed comfortably higher poll ratings than his rival Lafontaine. Such high ratings were crucial to Schröder's survival, given that it was his per-ceived popularity with the voters that had convinced SPD activists that he was the right candidate for Chancellor.

Schröder knew he had to assert his authority within the coalition and began briefing against his Finance Minister. On the Monday before Lafontaine's announcement, the tabloid newspaper *Bild* ran a front-page story condemning Lafontaine as the 'bogeyman' (*Buhmann*) of the coali-tion. Complete with unattributed quotes from 'government sources', the paper accused Lafontaine of provoking a flight of capital from Germany and undermining democracy by advocating co-operation with the PDS (*Bild*, 1 March 1999). Then, on the morning of Lafontaine's resignation, the paper ran another front-page exclusive, with the headline 'Schröder threatens resignation'. The paper described a row in Cabinet between the Chancellor and Lafontaine, where Schröder issued this ultimatum to his

Finance Minister: 'I won't allow myself to be associated with policies that are damaging to the economy … a point will come when I will no longer be able take responsibility for such policies' (*Bild*, 11 March 1999). The story obviously originated in the Chancellor's office and confirmed what insiders had known for quite a while, that Schröder and Lafontaine were increasingly unable to work together. One of them would have to go.

This was Schröder's last chance to rein-in his increasingly bold Finance Minister. Provoking a showdown was a calculated risk but Schröder undoubtedly hoped that, for Lafontaine, the moment of confrontation had come too early. However much Lafontaine coveted the Chancellorship, he knew that the coalition would not have survived a move against Schröder. Nor, after his public pronouncements, would the CDU/CSU or FDP have countenanced entering a government in which Lafontaine was Chancellor. Finally, such a move would not have been forgiven within the SPD itself. Lafontaine, a 'party man' to the core, had no choice but to resign. This was 'Schröder's second chance' (*Der Spiegel*, 15 March 1999).

Schröder soon took advantage of this second chance. Despite his expressions of surprise at Lafontaine's departure, Schröder moved quickly to consolidate his power. First, in recognition of the fragility of his position within his own party, he took over Lafontaine's position as SPD Chairman. Second, the vacant post of Finance Minister was given to Hans Eichel, the former Minister President of Hessen who had been defeated in the elections a month earlier. Eichel was a long-standing ally of Schröder and, in terms of temperament and politics, was the polar opposite of Lafontaine. Where Lafontaine was bold and overbearing, Eichel was cautious and collegiate and, for better or worse, lacked the charisma of his predecessor. Much in the same way as former British Prime Minister John Major, Eichel had built his reputation on his reputation for quiet competence rather grand political vision.[2] Crucially, however, Eichel enjoyed a reputation as a pro-business and fiscally orthodox politician with extensive networks within the worlds of business and finance. Having narrowly averted the much-predicted 'Red–Green chaos', the coalition desperately needed to re-build its credibility with these groups as a first step towards rehabilitating itself at home and abroad. It was some relief for the coalition when Wim Duisenberg pointedly approved of Eichel, saying 'I know him very well and congratulate Germany' (*Der Spiegel*, 15 March 1999).

The Kosovo crisis: Fischer's triumph

Once in office, Eichel immediately set about drawing up a radical pro-gramme of budgetary consolidation. Schröder, on the other hand, now had to turn his attention to the second major crisis of his administration – the war in Kosovo. The Kosovo crisis had been brewing since the previous summer. Before coming to office, Schröder and his Foreign Minister-designate Fischer had visited the USA. While in Washington, they reassured the Clinton administration of their support of NATO's threat of air-strikes if Milosevic moved against the ethnic Albanian majority in the troubled Serbian province (De-news, 10 October 1998). At the same time, Schröder and Fischer both knew that the Kosovo issue could not only break up the coalition but also divide German society as whole. As described earlier in the book, the Greens' ambivalent attitude towards the Federal Republic's defence arrangements had been regarded as a barrier to co-operation with the SPD at the Federal level. Although the reversal of the Greens proposed policy on withdrawal from NATO had overcome this obstacle, opposition to what was regarded as 'Western militarism' remained strong within the party. As a result, any German collusion in actual air-strikes could test to destruction the Greens' uneasy compromise on this issue. In addition, many politicians – and not just Greens – were highly critical of NATO's stance, given that it lacked a United Nations mandate (which had been blocked in the Security Council by Russia and China). Fischer's rival, Trittin, was particularly vocal in this respect. He argued that, without a UN mandate, NATO air-strikes would be in breach of international law (De-news, 13 October 1998).

Around this point in time, Milosevic climbed down in the face of inter-national pressure and NATO signed an agreement with the Yugoslav army to allow aerial surveillance of Kosovo. With the crisis apparently easing, the Kosovo issue became less heated and, on 17 October, the Bun-destag voted in favour of German participation in any future operations. Nevertheless, as Foreign Minister, Fischer remained in a difficult posi-tion. On the one hand, he held responsibility for maintaining the Federal Republic's 'Atlanticist' stance, which had been the cornerstone of German foreign policy in the post-war era and was regarded as crucial in per-suading the Bush administration to support German unity in 1989–90. On the other, however, he was the senior politician in a party with seri-ous misgivings about the planned NATO action. Unrest over German involvement in the Kosovo crisis also threatened to spill over into a more general feeling that Green involvement in the Federal coalition itself had been a mistake. This feeling had been further aggravated by Schröder's public humiliation of Trittin over the issue of nuclear reactors. Fischer had reason to fear that the Kosovo crisis would provide his opponents within the party with the opportunity to split with the SPD and retreat back into the comfortable certainties of opposition.

Eventually the Kosovo crisis erupted again and, on 24 March, NATO launched air-strikes against Yugoslav targets in Kosovo, Montenegro and Serbia. For the first time in post-war history, German guns fired in anger, with Luftwaffe pilots involved in targeting air-strikes and Bundeswehr troops stationed in Macedonia. Misgivings over involvement in military action was not just confined to the Greens. The left-wing of the SPD also opposed NATO action, including Lafontaine who belatedly claimed it as a reason for his sudden resignation a few weeks earlier. But the most important source of opposition to military involvement was the broadly pacifist general public in the Federal Republic. Germany's disastrous involvement in two world wars had instilled ordinary Germans with a profound horror of militarism. At the same time, support for Germany's Western alliances – including NATO – was reasonably solid, despite wide-spread opposition to the stationing of nuclear weapons on German soil during the cold war.

Obviously these two sentiments were contradictory. During the cold war era Germany was a 'semi-sovereign' state, content in many ways to play the role of 'economic giant' and 'political dwarf' (Bulmer and Paterson, 1987: 1). This limited conception of state sovereignty extended to the military sphere where, although Germany maintained a large conscript army, her strategic defence was effectively contracted-out to the USA. As a result, during this time it was not necessary for German elites to challenge this contradiction in public opinion. Ordinary Germans could free-ride under the American defence umbrella, content in the knowledge that they had exorcised the ghost of militarism from German soil. German elites and their international allies – both anxious to keep the genie of German power firmly in the bottle – were happy to let them do so. With German unification and the end of the cold war, the Federal Republic began to assume its share of collective security responsibilities. It became clear that the general public had to be conditioned to accept their country's new international status. The Bundeswehr was still restricted to the European theatre of operations, but areas of this theatre were increasingly unstable. The Federal Republic's retreat from military power was at an end, and public opinion had to change. But no-one would have anticipated that it would have had to be confronted with the prospect of a war in Europe in order to do so, nor that it would be a Green Foreign Minister who would argue that such a war was necessary.

Opinion polls indicated that Fischer would not find an easy political path through the Kosovo crisis. At the end of March, an Emnid poll indicated a deep public unease at NATO's action in the Balkans. More disturbingly, in a country still trying to recover from the effects of forty years of division, opinion differed considerably between those polled in the 'old' Federal Republic and those in the new states. For instance, in the West 64 per cent of the sample supported the NATO action and 69 per cent supported German involvement in it. This compared with only 39 per cent and 41 per cent in the East. However, a majority of respondents – 63 per cent and 74 per cent respectively – in both the West and East opposed the eventual use of NATO ground troops to solve the crisis (*Der Spiegel*, 29 March 1999). These and similar poll results elsewhere gave a clear message to Schröder and Fischer. Opinion was mixed on NATO air-strikes and could potentially be shifted in favour of it, but the use of ground troops – or at least Bundeswehr involvement in such a course of action – would be a step too far. The Chancellor and his Foreign Minister had to carry public opinion with them, and the parameters of public support for German participation in the Kosovo campaign were clearly limited.

Schröder and Fischer embarked on a double-edged strategy towards the Kosovo crisis, combining international statecraft with shrewd domestic political management. They had correctly calculated that the limited room for manouver they did possess lay on the diplomatic rather than military side of the crisis. Therefore, on the one hand, the Luftwaffe continued to participate in air-strikes and the number of Bundeswehr troops stationed in Macedonia was steadily increased. The appearance of unity within the NATO alliance was essential if Milosevic was to be coerced into reversing his policy of ethnic cleansing in the province and Germany could not be seen to be the weak link in this united front. At the same time, under the auspices of the Federal Republic's Presidency of the European Council, Fischer embarked on a hectic programme of shuttle diplomacy with the aim of brokering a deal which would get Milosevic and, increasingly, NATO off the hook. Schröder also took an active role, for instance talking to Russian Premier Primakov in Bonn at the beginning of April, but was careful to balance his diplomatic efforts with an unequivocal support of NATO military strategy. At the same time, political opposition to NATO action began to mobilise at home. The PDS predictably condemned Germany's involvement, with party leader Gregor Gysi declaring that he was 'ashamed for his country'. The Greens still officially supported NATO action, but opposition was growing within the party. The most high-profile dissenter within the Greens was Christian Ströbele, a veteran of the 1970s peace movements, who declared German support for the air strikes as a 'scandal' (*Der Spiegel*, 20 March 1999).

Although many experts had predicted a swift climb down by Milosevic, the NATO action continued into April. At the same time Milosevic escalated his policy of ethnic cleansing, creating a flood of Kosovar refugees who fled towards the borders with Macedonia, Montenegro and Bosnia. At home, public opinion shifted against NATO action. An Emnid poll in early April suggested that only 50 per cent of the population now supported continued air-strikes and 64 per cent now thought that they should be halted in order to pursue a diplomatic strategy (*Der Spiegel*, 5 April 1999). The reasons for this were fairly obvious. On the one hand, the sight of hundreds of thousands of refugees adrift in a war zone, and the tales of Serbian atrocities that they brought with them, stiffened the resolve of those involved to see the action through to its conclusion. It also allowed NATO to frame the action in the language of human rights and the liberation from tyranny. On the other hand, the bombing did not appear to be resolving the crisis and sometimes – as in the tragic attacks on a civilian passenger train and a convoy of refugees – appeared to aggravate it. Ordinary Germans had never wholeheartedly supported NATO action and now appeared to be revolted by it. Schröder and Fischer had to hope that NATO bombing would produce results very soon.

Responsibility for the domestic political management of the Kosovo crisis fell to an inner Cabinet of Schröder, Fischer, Defence Minister Scharping and Interior Minister Schilly. Scharping's involvement was obviously essential, but the inclusion of Schilly was an indicator of how seriously the government took the threat of civil unrest if the crisis continued. All four politicians keenly felt the historic weight of the crisis on their shoulders and none could have missed the irony of a Red–Green coalition leading Germany into its first armed action since the Second World War. As Chancellor, Schröder in particular was anxious to protect himself against accusations of war-mongering. 'Our decision to take action', he said 'was taken without any sign of jingoism', before making it clear that he 'was no war-Chancellor' (*Der Spiegel*, 12 April 1999).

At least Schröder, Scharping and Schilly could assure themselves that they had the broad support of their party. Over the years the SPD has had a long and noble tradition of pacifism but, on the surface at least, Social Democrats had closed ranks behind the leadership. Fischer, on the other hand, enjoyed no such luxury. Unlike the SPD, pacifism remained central to the Greens' core ideology and many within the party were now openly hostile to the Greens' continued participation in government. Fischer still retained a high degree of credibility with his party, as much because of his popularity with the general public as for his roots in the student protest movement of the late 1960s. But he knew that there were limits to how far he could push his party without triggering a backlash that would threaten his own position.

Opposition to NATO action inside the Greens took two forms. First, there were those members of the leadership who disapproved of the air strikes but were aware of how little room for manouver Fischer enjoyed. Some, such as Ströbele, were vocal in their opposition whilst others, such as Trittin and State Secretary Gila Altmann, were more circumspect in their pronouncements in public. These were the 'war sceptics' of the Green elite. There was also a second source of opposition who regarded the war as not just wrong in itself, but as more evidence of the Greens abandoning their principles in order to enter government. In essence, these were what remained of the party's fundamentalist wing. This latter group had no time for the measured opposition of Trittin and his colleagues. Indeed they regarded all those who continued to participate in the government as being warmongers by association, or 'olive-greens' as they called them. (Despite her own pacifism, unknown assailants sprayed 'warmonger' on the door of Altmann's office). The problem for Fischer was that such behaviour put pressure on the sceptics to harden their stance, which served to further limit his own room for manoeuvre. But Fischer had made it clear that he must be given that room if the Greens wanted to be taken seriously as a party of government. 'The Greens want to govern' he declared, and now 'they will be tempered in the fire … or burnt to ashes' (*Der Spiegel*, 12 April 1999).

As the NATO air campaign ground on through April, the Greens prepared for a special party conference on 13 May. The legacy of grass-roots democracy meant that the conference had the power to reject NATO action and, if necessary, force the party to leave the coalition. Fischer made it clear that if this happened he would leave the party, whilst Schröder declared that 'if the Greens don't play the game, I will find myself another partner' (*Der Spiegel*, 26 April 1999). Fischer's political career depended on his ability to convince the party to make one more concession to *realpolitik*. However, it now appeared that public opinion had shifted in the government's direction, with 41 per cent supporting continued NATO action and only 34 per cent still resolutely opposed (Emnid. 20–21 May 1999).

The 13 May conference was a stormy affair, but Fischer held his nerve. Despite barracking from some of the delegates, he gave an impassioned defence of the government's strategy – pointing out that Germany was at the forefront of diplomatic efforts to end the crisis. In the end the delegates voted in support of Fischer, but his victory was hard-won. While sitting next to Trittin, an anti-war activist ran towards the podium and threw a paint bomb at the Foreign Minister. The projectile hit Fischer on the side of head, perforating an ear-drum. Although obviously shaken, Fischer remained at his seat before later seeking medical attention.

Fischer's conference triumph signalled a turning of the political tide. At the same time, NATO was beginning to make progress in Kosovo. As May turned to June, it became clear that it was a question of when, rather than if, a diplomatic deal would be struck between the alliance and the Yugoslav army. At the same time, NATO's steady build-up of troops on Kosovo's borders continued. A full-scale land offensive would have probably been fatal for the Red–Green coalition, but Fischer was increasingly confident that it would not come to that. Finally, after seventy two days of NATO air strikes, a complicated 12-point plan was agreed between NATO and the Yugoslav army. The plan had been brokered under the aegis of the UN, and drawn up by the G8 group of industrialised nations and Yugoslav representatives. The outline plan was first announced by Foreign Ministers of the G8 and Russia few weeks earlier on 6 May and Fischer had been intimately involved in its inception. Key points included the establishment of buffer zones behind which Yugoslav troops would retreat and the return of all refugees to their homes. Crucially for Milosevic it also included the de-militarisation of the Kosovan Liberation Army (KLA) and the nominal retention of Kosovo as a Serbian province. Milosevic had been allowed to save some face. The G8 plan was ratified by the Serbian Parliament on 3 June 1999.

The successful resolution of the Kosovan crisis was an unalloyed success for the government. Schröder and Fischer had successfully executed a twin track strategy that had enhanced the status of Germany internationally and maintained the cohesion of the coalition at home. By both supporting NATO's military strategy and, at the same time, actively pursuing a diplomatic solution to the crisis the two men had resolved a potential conflict between the requirements of German statecraft (honouring the NATO commitment, etc.) and party politics (the need to prevent intra- and inter-party conflict within the coalition). Moreover, German public opinion had remained broadly supportive throughout. For Fischer, the resolution of the crisis was the end of a personal journey from outright pacifism which had begun when he had visited the site of the Srebrenica massacre in Bosnia in 1985. As he told an interviewer from *Der Spiegel*, until then he had opposed involvement in the Yugoslav wars of succession. However, the visit to Srebrenica had convinced him that 'Milosevic would carry on until he was stopped' (*Der Spiegel*, 21 June 1998). But a personal conversion from long-held beliefs was one thing, convincing an entire party to follow him was quite another. The ability of Fischer, as Foreign Minister, to carry the Greens with him and support Germany's first post-war involvement in military conflict was more than a political victory. It was a personal triumph.

Looking for the New Centre

The resolution of Kosovan crisis was also a triumph for Schröder. After months of drift and conflict, including the resignation of Lafontaine, he had re-asserted his authority over the coalition and established himself as an international statesman. All that was now required was a clear indication of where he wanted his government to go in policy terms. The fight against unemployment had not yet borne fruit and the coalition's nuclear and citizenship policies had both faltered. A pro-business attitude and commitment to balance the budget were all well and good, but 'Schröderism' – if there was such a thing – lacked a 'big idea'. Therefore the unveiling, in June 1999, of the British–German joint policy document on the 'Third Way', or 'New Centre', was greeted with anticipation.

As described earlier, the setting-up of the joint policy forum had been announced by Schröder and Blair in London in late 1998. Although the publication of the Blair–Schröder document had been delayed by the Kosovo crisis, leaks in both countries had prepared the ground for its publication and it was widely expected it would be an unashamedly 'modernising' document. In this respect, at least, it was not to disappoint. The document attempted to reconcile the social democratic tradition with the contemporary neo-liberal orthodoxy. This was made clear in the preamble to the document which declared that 'social democracy has found new acceptance … because it stands not only for social justice but also for economic dynamism and the unleashing of creativity and innovation'. Social Democratic governments had to embark on a process of 'modernisation', in order to adapt 'to conditions that have objectively changed'. In future, 'the State should not row, but steer: not so much control as challenge'. There also had to be a 'new supply-side agenda for the left' with the aim of 'catching up with the US'. Governments had to establish a 'robust and competitive market framework' with a 'tax policy to promote sustainable growth' at its core. The weapons in the modernisers armoury were to include simpler and lighter corporate taxation, shifting the tax burden from income to consumption, tax relief and lower starting rates of income tax. More contentiously in a German context, there had to be greater 'flexibility' in the labour market (SPD, 1999). The document proposed that this would be achieved by the reduction of non-wage labour costs and the promotion of small and medium-sized enterprises, both of which were uncontroversial but had proved difficult to achieve. However, the suggestion to extend welfare-to-work policies was more controversial in the context of the Federal Republic.[4]

The paper was greeted with some scepticism in both Germany and Britain. In the UK the paper was regarded as being a little lightweight but, in the Federal Republic, reaction was far more hostile. Many saw it as a blatant attack on the Rhineland model of social market capitalism. The idea of the 'New Centre' was not new one – Schröder had first used the phrase during his campaign to be nominated as Chancellor-candidate. But until the publication of the joint policy document, the Chancellor had never really fleshed out his ideas in detail. Schröder's ally Bodo Hombach had written a book on the subject which had argued along similar lines to the policy document, but Hombach was not such a high profile figure and had by this time resigned as Minister to the Chancellor's Office. The Blair–Schröder document had little visible support within the academy either. Schröder's circle were keen to associate themselves with the ideas of Anthony Giddens (1998) and Ulrich Beck (1998), whose work developing 'Third Way' ideas had had a substantial impact in both Germany and Britain. But elsewhere academic opinion was either hostile in principle (see Dörre 1999) or sceptical about the possibility of a 'Blairite' agenda successfully transferring to the quite different structures and norms of the Federal Republic (Lees, in Martell *et al.*, 2001).

The Blair–Schröder document promoted a top-down, elite-driven agenda, to which traditional Social Democrats and trade unionists reacted with shock *Der Spiegel* called it an attempt to a execute a 'Bad Godesberg from above' (*Der Spiegel*, 14 June 1999).[5] However, with the departure of Lafontaine, the SPD left lacked a figurehead around which to mobilise opposition. Nevertheless, there remained a palpable unease within the party, summed up by the words of a party activist who complained that 'somehow everything has gone wrong since the election' (ibid.). The dispirited mood within the party was deepened further over the summer and early autumn of 1999. Shortly after the publication of the Blair–Schröder document, the SPD performed badly in elections to the European Parliament. It did not escape the notice of SPD activists that Blair's Labour party suffered a similar set-back, nor that the only European Social Democratic party to perform well in the elections was Jospin's unreformed PS. The electorate appeared to have delivered its judgement on the Third Way!

Of course, the truth was more complicated than that. Just like the Labour party in the UK, the SPD's poor showing owed much to non-voting. The Federal Republic has a historically high turnout in European elections and the 1999 turnout of 45.2 per cent was regarded by many as a signal of popular disenchantment with the overall performance of the Red–Green coalition, rather than the New Centre agenda. This perception was reinforced just after the European elections by an Emnid poll which indicated that 46 per cent of non-voters abstained for this reason (*Der Spiegel*, 21 June 1999). Over the next few months, popular disenchantment with the coalition was further demonstrated by the SPD's poor showing in state elections in Berlin and Bremen. By October, national polling indicated that the CDU/CSU had opened up a 14 point gap over the SPD. Schröder's standing within the SPD – which had never been secure – now looked perilous and there were rumours that Scharping might move against him at the party's December 1999 conference in Berlin. These rumours came to nothing. But the Chancellor – ever the pragmatist – began to distance himself from the Blair–Schröder paper. In October, SPD news managers began to make it clear that Schröder was prepared to ditch the document. Apparently Schröder now realised that neo-liberal prescriptions were not suitable to conditions in the Federal Republic. Reforms were still necessary, but there were other models to consider, such as in The Netherlands and – more importantly – France. Schröder's new course was to be 'more Jospin and less Blair' (*Der Spiegel*, 18 October 1999: 23). The New Centre remained as elusive as ever.

Notes

1 The group first met on 7 December 1998 and issued a 'common statement' setting out the structures described here.
2 During the Hessen election campaigns the previous month, Schröder had personally campaigned for Eichel and praised his low-profile approach. Eichel, said Schröder, was a safe pair of hands, even though he 'doesn't dance like Fred Astaire or sing like Caruso'!
3 A reference to the colour of German battlefield dress.

4 The document also stressed the idea of EU-level co-operation as a means to disseminate this new agenda, albeit using the private-sector metaphor of 'political benchmarking'. This benchmarking process would have three elements. First, there would be a series of Ministerial meetings and an ongoing process of staff liaison between Britain and Germany. Second, Blair and Schröder would 'seek discussion' with political leaders in other EU countries, regardless of political affiliation. Third, they would promote the establishment of a 'network of experts, farsighted thinkers, political fora and discussion meetings' which would 'deepen and continually further develop the concept of the New Centre and the Third Way'.

5 A reference to the 1956 Bad Godesberg programme that re-oriented the SPD as a catch-all party.

9

Conclusion

Schröder's record as Chancellor

Successful politicians need a little luck occasionally and Gerhard Schröder is a very lucky politician indeed. In October 1999, his Chancellorship appeared to be on the rocks. Yet, two months later he secured a standing ovation at the SPD's December conference and his party was ahead in the polls. How had this change of affairs come about?

In November 1999, the CDU was plunged into a scandal over the misuse and non-declaration of secret party accounts. Among those implicated were former Chancellor Kohl and his successor as CDU leader, Wolfgang Schauble, as well as other senior politicians. The scandal gathered momentum over the next few months and the Chancellor's own troubles – including a number of less significant money scandals involving his own party – faded from the public eye. But Schröder's rehabilitation was also the result of his distancing himself from the Blair–Schröder paper. At the time of the policy document's publication, some commentators began to portray the Chancellor as a neo-liberal ideologue determined to force his programme through despite the opposition of his party and much of the general population. For someone who had made a career out of pragmatism and populism this portrayal must have come as a shock to Schröder. He may have found the Blairite agenda attractive in general terms, but his reputation as a 'moderniser' was built on little more than rhetoric. During the battle with Lafontaine for the nomination as Chancellor-candidate, such a reputation was useful to Schröder. It served to distance him from the SPD left and appeal to middle-class voters who found Lafontaine's brand of social democracy unattractive. Such an approach also complemented the message of the SPD's Bundestag election campaign, with its emphasis on the vague idea of 'innovation'.

The record of Schröder's eight years as Minister President of Nieder-sachsen reveals no evidence of a Blairite in the making. Even when the SPD ruled alone, between 1994 and 1998, the party's policy record was fairly unspectacular. The state suffered from structural decline – brought on by an over-reliance on heavy industry and agriculture – and the main priority of any state government was tackling unemployment. There were one or two high profile initiatives, such as the re-location of the Daimler-Benz test-track and the bailing out of the DASA concern, but the general thrust of policy was reactive and path-dependent. On 24 November 1999, this side of Schröder's character re-emerged when he approved the use of Federal funds to bale out the struggling 'Holzmann' building concern.

The sight of Schröder accepting the applause of a crowd of hard-hatted trade unionists was more reminiscent of an 'old' SPD party boss than a cutting-edge moderniser. But this is part of the Schröder enigma. Those who have worked with Schröder have no illusions that he is anything more than a pro-business SPD right-winger with corporatist instincts. Even senior Greens complain that he 'talks like a reformer, but behaves like a traditionalist' (*Der Spiegel*, 14 June 1999). But politics is the art of the possible. Schröder does not control his party in the way that Blair does. Even if he did, the system of multi-level governance in the Federal Republic has so many checks and balances built into that he would still have to work with the grain of a system that is highly resistant to change. Even Helmut Kohl, with his formidable powerbase within the CDU, failed to address the need for fundamental reform.

Nevertheless, Schröder's first year as Chancellor was not impressive. The only real success, which should not be under-rated, was the prosecu-tion of the Kosovo campaign. Here he owes much to his Foreign Minister Joschka Fischer. Otherwise, the general impression has been one of bad political management, intra- and inter-party strife. In policy terms, none of the coalition's stated main objectives have been achieved. Unemploy-ment remains stubbornly high and the Alliance for Jobs has yet to bear fruit. A timetable for the planned withdrawal from the use of nuclear power is yet to be achieved, although consensus talks go on. And the orig-inal plan for citizenship law reform has been watered down and replaced by a more limited set of reforms, with the agreement of the opposition parties. Schröder remains in power, but the euphoria of Autumn 1998 is a thing of the past.

Evaluating Red–Green coalitions

It must not be forgotten that Schröder did not want a Red–Green coalition. Before the election he had made it clear that a Grand Coalition would have given him the necessary room to out-manouvere Lafontaine and the SPD's left wing. Only then, it was argued, would the government be able to introduce the supply-side reforms necessary to make a real impact on unemployment. Yet, with the resignation of Oskar Lafontaine, the SPD's left lacks a focus and is not in a position to oppose such reforms at present. So why is Schröder still constrained? Could it be the Greens?

In Chapter 2 I suggested political co-operation between the SPD and Greens has generated an 'ideal type' (Lees, 1999) or 'Red–Green model'. This model was developed over time, using the institutional knowledge built up during the period of co-operation at the sub-national level. This ideal type relied on the successful resolution of three sets of issues. First, the parties had to selectively emphasise compatible elements in their respective ideological stances and, over time, they learnt to 'flag' them in their election programmes. The SPD learnt to talk up its post-materialist dimension and stress 'quality-of-life' issues, whilst the Greens had to do the opposite – and moderate those elements of their profile that distanced them from the political mainstream. In particular they had to finally accept consumer capitalism and, crucially, the state's monopoly on legitimate force and its external defence arrangements. The extent to which this has been achieved can be judged by the coalition's success in dealing with the Kosovan crisis. Second, over time the two parties developed a path-dependent pattern of portfolio allocation. The SPD regarded ownership of 'core' portfolios like Finance, Economics and Industry as non-negotiable, in return for which the Greens would expect the Environment portfolio, preferably with both the Ministerial and State Secretary posts. Finally, the Greens had to deal with the problem of staffing this Ministry. No doubt there was no shortage of environmental expertise available to the party, but did these individuals possess enough political experience to make the transition to government? Trittin's nuclear debacle in the first months suggests that the Greens remain at a disadvantage in this respect.

Over time, the Greens will close this expertise gap. The longer they remain in power, the more they will be able to open up existing policy networks to their client groups, as well as socialise their own personnel into the business of national government. The question remains if they can succeed in doing this without losing their radical edge and, on the evidence of the first year of the Schröder administration, this might be difficult. It will take more than what has so far been achieved to convince their own supporters that the 'Long March through the Länder' has indeed been worth the effort.

For the SPD, the long years out of power at the Federal level are over. The party remains notoriously hard to lead and the ideological ambiguity that has characterised it since the 1970s has not yet been resolved. Indeed, this 'janus faced' ideological profile may be an advantage. Co-operation with the Greens arose out of electoral necessity and many in the party are aware that such arrangements are perhaps better suited to the relatively risk-free environment of the state-level of governance. Given the chance, they might opt for a Grand Coalition or even an SPD–FDP alliance – subject to calculations about the trade-off between office-seeking and policy-oriented goals. At present, however, the SPD can conceivably enter into a Federal coalition with any of the three other mainstream parties and, in the new states of the East, even with the PDS. In a party system were coalition government is the norm, the SPD has more options than most.

And what of Schröder? All the evidence suggests that he has no great commitment to the idea of the Red–Green coalition. Indeed, the experience of Niedersachsen suggests that he would jettison them if he could. But Schröder knows that at present he must make the Red–Green coalition work, even though the template on which it is based is essentially a sub-national one. As the coalition enters its second year, Schröder finds himself in a stronger position than he might have expected a few months before. The SPD's left-wing is temporarily demoralised, the Greens remain passive and the CDU is tearing itself apart. Throughout his career, Schröder has demonstrated an ability to make the most of difficult political circumstances.It remains to be seen if Schröder rises to the challenge he now faces.

Bibliography

Abgeordnetenhaus von Berlin (1991), Plenarprotokollen, Band I, 1989, 1 bis 18 Sitzung.

Abgeordnetenhaus von Berlin (1991), Plenarprotokollen, Band II, 1989/1990, 19 bis 31 Sitzung.

Abgeordnetenhaus von Berlin (1991), Plenarprotokollen, Band III, 1990, 32 bis 50 Sitzung.

Achimer Kreiszeitung newspaper.

Aguilar, S. (1993), 'Corporatist and statist designs in environmental policy: The contrasting roles of Germany and Spain in the European Community scenario', *Environmental Politics*, 2, 2: 223–47.

Altenstetter, C. (1994) 'European Union responses to Aids/HIV and policy networks in the pre-Maastricht era', *Journal of European Public Policy*, 1, 3: 413–40.

Alternative Liste Berlin (AL) (1989), *Das Kurzprogramme der Aternativen Liste. Die Kandidatinnen und Kandidaten für das Abgeordnetenhaus.*

Alternative Berlin Liste (AL) (1991), *Rechenschaftsbericht der Fraktion Grüne/ Alternativen Liste Berlin 1989/1990.*

Austen-Smith, A. and Banks, J. (1988), 'Elections, coalitions and legislative outcomes', *American Political Science Review*, 82: 405–22.

Axelrod, R. (1970), *Conflict of Interest*, (Chicago: Markham).

Bacharach, M. (1976), *Economics and the Theory of Games* (Basingstoke: Macmillan).

Batley, R. and Stoker, G. (1991), *Local Government in Europe: Trends and Developments*, (Basingstoke: Macmillan).

Beck, U. (1998), *Politik der Globalisierung* (Frankfurt a.m: Suhrkamp).

Benson, J. K. (1982), 'A framework for policy analysis', in Rogers, D. *et al.*, (eds) *Interorganisational Co-ordination* (Ames: Iowa State University Press).

Berlau, A. J. (1949), *The German Social Democratic Party, 1914–1921* (New York: Columbia University Press).

Berliner Statistik. Statistische Berichte (1989). *Wahlen in Berlin (West) am 29 Jan-*

uar 1989. *Endgültiges Ergebnis der Wahlen zum Abgeordnetenhaus und zu den Bezirksverordnetenversammlungen*, Statistisches Landesamt Berlin.

Bickerich, W. (ed.) (1985), *SPD und Grüne: Das neue Bündnis?* (Hamburg: Spiegel-Buch).

Bild magazine.

Bildzeitung newspaper.

Black, D. (1958), *The Theory of Committees and Elections* (Cambridge: Cambridge University Press).

Blanke, B. *et al.* (1996), '*Modernisierung' des Staates? Öffentliche Aufgaben und Wettbewerb, Transformation des Sozialstaates, ökologischer Umbau, Europäischer Perspektiven.* Hannover: Abteilung Sozialpolitik und Public Policy, Universität Hannover. Forschungsbericht Nr. 2.

Blondel, J. (1968), 'Party systems and patterns of government in western democracies', *Canadian Journal of Political Science*, 1: 180–203. Reprinted in Wolinetz, S. B. (ed.) (1998) *Party Systems* (Aldershot: Dartmouth).

Blühdorn, I. and Krause, F. (eds) (1995), *Environmental Politics and Policy in Germany* (Keele: Keele University Press).

Boehmer-Christiansen, S. and Skea, J. (1991), *Acid Politics* (Toronto: Belhaven House).

Bogdanor, V. (ed.) (1983), *Coalition Government in Western Europe* (London: Heinemann).

Braunschweiger Zeitung newspaper.

Browne, E., Gleiber, D. and Mashoba, C. (1984), 'Evaluating conflict of interest theory: western European cabinet coalitions, 1945–80', *British Journal of Political Science*, 28: 671–92.

Browne, E. C. (1973), *Coalition Theories: A Logical And Empirical Critique* (Newbury Park: Sage).

Budge, I. and Keman, H. (1990), *Parties and Democracy: Coalition Formation and Government Functioning in Twenty States* (Oxford: Oxford University Press).

Budge, I., Robertson, D. and Hearl, D. (eds) (1987), *Ideology, Strategy and Party Change: Spatial Analyses of Post-War Election Programmes In 19 Democracies* (Cambridge: Cambridge University Press).

Bulmer, S. and Paterson, W. (1987), *The Federal Republic of Germany and the European Community* (London: Allen & Unwin).

Bulmer, S. (1983), 'Domestic politics and European Community policy making', *Journal of Common Market Studies*, 21, 4: 349–63.

Bündnis 90/Die Grünen (1995), *Koalitionsverienbarung Für Die 14. Wahlperiode Des Hessischen Landtags Zwischen Bündnis 90/Die Grünen & SPD 1995–1999.*

Bündnis 90/Die Grünen (1995), *Landtagswahlprogramm, Hessenn '95.*

Bündnis 90/Die Grünen (1996), 'Reform der Niedersächsischen Umweltverwaltung'. Internal Discussion Document (limited circulation).

Bündnis 90/Die Grünen (1998), *Grün ist der Wechsel. Programm zur Bundestagswahl 98.*

Bündnis 90/Die Grünen Pressestelle (various), *Pressespiegel: Artikel mit Nennung von Bündnis 90/Die Grünen.*

Bürklin, W. and Roth, D. (eds) (1993), *Das Superwahljahr: Deutschland vor unkalkulierbaren Regierungsmehrheiten* (Cologne: Bund Verlag).

Carson, R. (1962), *Silent Spring* (Boston: Houghton Mifflin).

CDU Landesverband Niedersachsen (1990), *Wahlprogramme 1990. Ein Starkes Niedersachsen im Herzen Deutschlands.*

CDU/CSU (1998), *1998–2002 Wahl-platform.*

Cellesche Zeitung newspaper.

Cerny, K. H. (ed.) (1990), *Germany at the Polls: The Bundestag Elections of the 1980s* (Durham, NC: Duke University Press).

Chandler, J. A. (ed.) (1993), *Local Government In Liberal Democracies.* (London: Routledge).

Colomer, J. M. and Martinez, F. (1995), 'The paradox of coalition trading'. *Journal of Theoretical Politics*, 7, 1: 41–63.

Crewe, I. and Denver, D. (1985), *Electoral Change in Western Democracies, Patterns and Sources of Electoral Volatility* (London: Croom Helm).

Dalton, R. (1992), 'Two German electorates?', in Smith, G. *et al* (eds), *Developments in German Politics* (Basingstoke: Macmillan).

Dalton, R. *et al.* (1984), *Electoral Change in Advanced Industrial Democracies* (Princeton, Guildford: Princeton University Press).

de Swaan, A. (1973), *Coalition Theories and Cabinet Formation* (Amsterdam, Oxford: Elsevier).

Delwaide, J. (1993), 'Postmaterialism and politics: the "Schmidt SPD" and the greening of Germany', *German Politics*, 2, 2.

De-news@listserv.gmd.de

Denzau and Mackay (1987), 'Structure induced equilibrium', in Baron, D. and Ferejohn, J. (eds) 'Bargaining in Legislatures'. Stanford, CA: Stanford University (unpublished).

Dodd, L. C. (1976), *Coalitions in Parliamentary Government*, (Princeton, Guildford: Princeton University Press).

Döring, Herbert and Smith, Gordon (eds) (1982), *Party Government and Political Culture in Western Germany* (Basingstoke: Macmillan).

Dörre, K., Panitch, L., Zeuner, B., u.a. (1999), *Die Strategie der 'Neuen Mitte'. Verabschiedet sich der moderne Sozialdemokratie als Reformpartei?* (Hamburg: VSA-Verlag).

Downs, A. (1957), *An Economic Theory of Democracy* (New York: Harper and Row).

Downs, W. M. (1998), *Coalition Government Subnational Style: Multiparty Politics in Europe's Regional Parliaments* (Columbus: Ohio State University Press).

Dreyhaupt, F., Dierschke ,W., Kropp, L., Prinz, B. and Schade, H. (1979), *Handbuch zur Aufstellung von Luftreinhalteplänen. Entwicklung und Ziele regionaler Luftreinhaltestrategie* (Mainz: TÜV Rheinland GmbH).

Dunleavy, P. (1991), *Democracy, Bureaucracy and Public Choice* (Hemel Hempstead: Harvester/Wheatsheaf).

Dyson, K. (ed.) (1992), *The Politics of German Regulation* (Aldershot: Dartmouth).

Eckersley, R. (1989), 'Green politics and the new class: Selfishness or virtue?', *Political Studies*, 37: 205–23.

Edinger, L. J. (1956), *German Exile Politics. The Social Democratic Executive Committee in the Nazi Era* (Berkeley, CA: University of California Press).

Eilfort, M. (1995), 'Politikverdrossenheit and the non-voter', in Roberts, G. (ed.), *Superwahljahr: The German Elections in 1994* (London: Frank Cass).

The European newspaper.

Feld, W. J. (ed.) (1978), *The Foreign Policies of West European Socialist Parties* (New York, London: Praeger).

Flockton, C. (1993), 'The Federal German economy in the early 1990s'. *German Politics*, 2.

Focus, Wahl-Spezial/1998.

Focus magazine.

FORSA. Gesellschaft für Sozialforschung und statistische Analysen mbH (1993), Opinion Poll Report.

Forschungsgruppe Wahlen (1990/1994/1990).

Die Frankfurter Allgemeine Zeitung (FAZ) newspaper.

Frankland, E. G. and Schoomaker, D. (1992), *Between Protest and Power: The Green Party in Germany* (Boulder: Westview Press).

Freeman, G. (1983), 'National styles and policy sectors: explaining structured variation', *Journal of Public Policy*, 5, 4: 467–96.

FDP Landesverband Niedersachsen (1990), *Freiheit hat Zukunft*, Landtagswahlprogramme Gesamtausgabe.

Friedman, M. (1953), *Essays in Positive Economics* (Chicago: University of Chicago Press).

Friedman, M. (1966), 'The methodology of positive economics', in Friedman, M. (ed.), *Essays in Positive Economics* (Chicago: University of Chicago Press).

Gamson, W. A. (1961), 'A theory of coalition formation', *American Sociological Review*, 26: 373–82.

Giddens, A. (1982), *Profiles and Critiques in Social Theory* (Basingstoke: Macmillan).

Giddens, A. (1984), *The Constitution of Society: Outline of the Theory of Structuration* (Cambridge: Polity Press).

Giddens, A. (1998), *The Third Way: The Renewal of Social Democracy* (Cambridge: Polity Press).

Gilligan, T. and Krehbiel, K. (1987), 'Collective decision making and standing committees: an informational rationale for restrictive amendment procedure', *Journal of Law, Economics and Organisations*, 3: 287–335.

Goldberger, B. (1993), 'Why Europe should not fear the Germans', *German Politics*, 2.

Grant, W., Paterson, W. and Whitson, C. (1988), *Government and the Chemical Industry: A Comparative Study of Britain and West Germany* (Oxford: Clarendon Press).

Green, S. (1995), 'All change? The German party system and the aftermath of Superwahljahr', Birmingham: Institute for German Studies Working Paper, IGS95/5, University of Birmingham.

Groennings, S., Kelly, E. W. and Leiserson, M. (1970), *The Study of Coalition Behaviour: Theoretical Perspectives and Cases from Four Continents* (New York, London: Holt, Rinehart & Winston).

Grofman, B. (1982), 'A dynamic model of protocoalition formation in ideological *n*-space', *Behavioural Science*, 27: 77–90.

Die Grünen Landesverband Niedersachsen (1990). *Die Grünen. Programme '90.*

Die Welt newspaper.

Grüne Zeiten magazine.

Handelsblatt newspaper.

Hannoversche Allgemeine Zeitung (HAZ) newspaper.

Hanson, R. A. (1972), '*Majority rule and policy outcomes: A critique of the calculus of consent*', Ph.D. Thesis, Minneapolis: University of Minnesota.

Hanson, R. A. and Rice, P. M. (1972), 'Committees, representation and policy outcomes', *Annals of the NY Academy of Sciences.*

Hargreaves-Heap, S. *et al.* (1992), *The Theory Of Choice: A Critical Guide*, (Oxford: Blackwell).

Harmel, R. and Janda, K. (1994), 'An integrated theory of party goals and party change', *Journal Of Theoretical Politics*, 6: 259–87.

Heinrich, G. (1993), *Rot-Grün in Berlin*. Marburg: Schüren.

Hinckley, B. (1981), *Coalitions and Politics* (London: Harcourt Brace Jovanovich).

HM Treasury Press Office.

Hübner, E. and Oberreuter, H. (eds) (1992), *Parteien in Deutschland zwischen Kontinuität und Wandel* (Munich: Bayerische Landeszentrale für politische Bildungsarbeit).

Hülsberg, W. (1988), *The German Greens: A Social and Political Profile* (London: Verso).

Hunt, R. N. (1964), *German Social Democracy 1918–1933* (New Haven: Yale University Press).

Inglehart, R. (1990), *Culture Shift in Advanced Industrial Society* (Princeton; Guildford: Princeton University Press).

Irving, R. E. M. (date unavailable), 'Christian Democracy in post-war Europe: Conservatism writ-large or distinctive political phenomenon?', *West European Politics.*

Janda, K., Harmel, R., Edens, C. and Goff, P. (1995), 'Changes in party identity: Evidence from party manifestos', *Party Politics*, 1, 2: 171–96.

Jänicke, M. (1990), *State Failure* (Cambridge: Polity Press).

Jänicke, M. (1992), 'Conditions for environmental policy success: an international comparison', *The Environmentalist*, 12, 1: 47–58.

Jeffery, C. and Lees, C. (1998), 'Whither the old order? The collapse of the GDR and the "new" German party system', in P. Davies and J. White (eds), *Political Parties and the Collapse of Old Orders* (SUNY Press).

Jeffery, C. (1994), 'The Länder strike back: Structures and procedures of European integration policy making in the German federal system', Discussion Papers In Federal Studies FS94/4, Centre for Federal Studies, University of Leicester.

Jordan, G. and Schubert, K. (1992), 'A preliminary ordering of policy network labels'. *European Journal of Political Research*, 21, 1–2: 7–29.

Jun, U. (1994), *Koalitionsbildung in den deutschen Bundesländern. Theoretische Betrachtungen, Dokumentation und Analyse* (Opladen: Leske und Budrich).

Katz, R. and Mair, P. (eds) (1992), *Party Organisations: A Data Hand-Book on Party Organisations in Western Democracies* (Newbury Park: Sage).

Katz, R. and Mair, P. (1995), 'Changing models of party organisation and party democracy: the emergence of the Cartel Party', *Party Politics*, 1, 1: 5–28.

Katzenstein, P. J. (1987), *Policy and Politics in West Germany: The Growth of a Semi-Sovereign State* (Philadelphia: Temple University Press).

Katzenstein, P. J. (1989), *Industry and Politics in West Germany: Towards the Third Republic* (Ithaca: Cornell University Press).

Kirchheimer, O. (1966), 'The transformation of the Western European party systems', in La Palombara, J. and Wiener, M. (eds), *Political Parties and Political Development* (Princeton, Guildford: Princeton University Press).

Kitschelt, H. (1989), *The Logics Of Party Formation: Ecological Politics in Belgium and West Germany* (Ithaca: Cornell University Press).

Kitschelt, H. (1986), 'Political opportunity structures and political protest: Antinuclear movements in four democracies', *British Journal of Political Science*, 16,1.

Kleinert, H. (1992), *Aufstieg und Fall der Grünen: Analyse einer alternativen Partei* (Bonn: Verlag J. H. W. Dietz Nachf).

Kolinsky, E. (ed.) (1989), *The Greens in West Germany* (Oxford: Berg).

Krehbiel, K. (1988), 'Spatial models of legislative choice', *Legislative Studies Quarterly*, 3: 259–319.

Ladrech, R. (1994), 'Europeanisation of domestic politics and institutions: The case of France', *Journal of Common Market Studies*, 32, 1: 69–88.

Landfried, C. (1994), 'The judicialisation of politics in Germany', *International Political Science Review*, 15, 2: 113–24.

Laver, M. (1979), *Playing Politics* (Harmondsworth: Penguin Books).

Laver, M. and Schofield, N. (1990), *Multi-Party Government: The Politics of Coalition in Europe* (Oxford: Oxford University Press).

Lees, C. (1995), 'Paradise postponed: An assessment of ten years of governmental participation by the German Green party', Discussion paper, IGS95/4, Institute for German Studies, University of Birmingham.

Lees, C. (1996a), 'A watershed election: The Berlin state and city elections of 22 October 1995', *Regional and Federal Studies*, 6, 1: 63–72.

Lees, C. (1996b), 'The ambivalent Left: The Greens, the PDS and the SPD's strategic dilemma', *Contemporary Political Studies*, 3: 1438–51.

Lees, C. (1998), 'Red–Green Coalitions in the Federal Republic of Germany: Models of Formation and Maintenance', Doctoral Thesis, University of Birmingham.

Lees, C. (1999), 'The Red–Green coalition', in Padgett, S. and Saalfield, T. (eds), *Bundestagswahl: '98: The End of an Era* (London: Frank Cass).

Lees, C. (2001), 'The Third Way and the Neue Mitte: How institutional structures and norms constrain political innovation', in Martell *et al.* (eds), *Social Democracy: Current Directions* (Basingstoke: Macmillan).

Lehmbruch, G. and Schmitter, P. (eds) (1982), *Patterns of Corporatist Policy Making* (Newbury Park: Sage).

Lehmbruch, G. (1989), 'Institutional linkages and policy networks in the federal system of West Germany', *Publius*, 19, 4: 221–35.

Lehmbruch, G. (1992), 'The institutionalisation of German regulation', in Dyson, K. (ed.), *The Politics of German Regulation* (Aldershot: Dartmouth).

Leiserson, M. (1968), 'Factions and coalitions in one-party Japan', *American Political Science Review*, 68: 770–87.

Lipinski, R. (1927–28), *Die Sozialdemokratie von ihren Anfängen bis zur Gegenwart*, Vols. I and II. SPD Berlin.

Lipset, S. and Rokkan, S. (1967), *Party Systems and Voter Alignments: Cross-National Perspectives* (New York: Free Press).

Lijphart, A. (1971), 'Comparative politics and the comparative method', *American Political Science Review*, 65: 652–93.

Lodge, J. (ed.) (1990), *The 1989 Election of the European Parliament* (Basingstoke: Macmillan).

Mackie, T. and Marsh, D. (1995), 'The comparative method', in Marsh, D. and Stoker, G. (eds), *Theory and Methods in Political Science* (Basingstoke: Macmillan).

Mair, P. (ed.) (1990), *The West European Party System* (Oxford: Oxford University Press).

Mair, P. and Smith, G. (eds) (1990), *Understanding Party System Change in Western Europe* (London: Frank Cass).

Markovits, A. S. and Gorski, P. S. (1993), *The German Left: Red, Green and Beyond* (Cambridge: Polity Press).

Marsh, D. (1983), *Pressure Politics* (London: Junction Books).

Mattox, G. A. and Bradley Shingleton, A. (eds) (1992), *Germany at the Crossroads: Foreign and Domestic Policy Issues* (Boulder, CO: Westview Press).

Mehring, F. (1897), *Geschichte der deutschen Sozialdemokratie*, Vols. I–IV (Berlin: Dietz).

Merkl, P. (ed.) (1980), *Western European Party Systems* (New York: Free Press).

Merkl, P. (ed.) (1989), *The Federal Republic of Germany at Forty* (New York: New York University Press).

Mettke, J. R. (1982), *Die Grünen: Regierungspartner von morgen?* (Hamburg: Spiegel-Buch).

Michels, R. (1970), *Zur Sociologie des Parteiwesens in der modernen Demokratie* (Berlin, Leipzig, Stuttgart: Union Deutsche Verlagsgesellschaft).

Mintzel A. and Oberreuter, H. (eds) (1992), *Parteien in der Bundesrepublik Deutschsland* (Bonn: Bundeszentrale für politische Bildung).

Moravcsik, A. (1994), 'Why the European Union strengthens the State: Domestic politics and international co-operation', Working Paper 52, Centre for European Studies, Harvard University, Cambridge, MA.

Müller, E. (1989), 'Sozial-liberale Umweltpolitik, Von der Karriere eines neuen Politikbereichs', *Aus Politik und Zeitgeschichte*, B 47–48: 3–15.

Müller, E-P. (date unavailable), *Die Grünen und das Parteiensystem* (Cologne: Deutscher Instituts-Verlag).

Müller, E-P. (1990), *Das Berliner Programme der SPD* (Cologne: Deutsche Instituts-Verlag).

Müller-Rommel, F. (1993), *Grüne Parteien in Westeuropa: Entwicklungsphasen und Erfolgsbedingungen* (Opladen: Westdeutscher Verlag).

Müller-Rommel, F. and Poguntke, T. (1992), 'Die Grünen', in Mintzel, A. and Oberreuter, H. (eds), *Parteien in der Bundesrepublik Deutschland* (Opladen: Leske and Buderich).

Neue Presse newspaper.

Niedersächsisches UmweltMinisterium (1995), *Kommission der Niedersächsischen Landesregierung zur Vermeidung und Verwertung von Reststoffen und Abfällen. Gesamtabschlußbericht einschl. der Berichte der Arbeitskreise.*

Niedersächsisches Umweltministerium (1995), *Beirat für Fragen des Kernenergieaussteigs (BfK), Tätigkeitbericht für den Zeitraum Dezember 1991 bis Dezember 1995.*

Niedersächsisches Ministerium für Bundes- und Europaangelegenheiten (various). *Pressespiegel.*

Nordsee Zeitung newspaper.

Nullmeier, F. (1989), 'Institutionelle Innovation und neue soziale Bewegungen', *Aus Politik und Zeitgesichte*, B26/89.

Oldenburgische Volkszeitung newspaper.

Ostfriesen Zeitung newspaper.

Ostfriesische Nachtrichten newspaper.

Padgett, S. and Burkett, T. (1986), *Political Parties and Elections in Western Germany* (London: Hurst/St. Martins).

Padgett, S. and Paterson, W. (1991), 'The rise and fall of the German Left', *New Left Review*, 186.

Padgett, S. (1993a), 'The new German electorate', in Padgett, S. (ed.), *Parties and Party Systems in the New Germany* (Aldershot: Dartmouth).

Padgett, S. (1993b), 'The German Social Democrats: A re-definition of social democracy or Bad Godesburg Mark II?', in Gillespie, R. and Paterson, W. E. (eds), *Rethinking Social Democracy in Europe* (London: Frank Cass).

Page, E. (1991), *Localism and Centralism in Europe* (Oxford: Oxford University Press).

Page, E. and Goldsmith, M. (eds) (1987), *Central and Local Government Relations: A Comparative Analysis of West European Unitary States* (Newbury Park: Sage).

Panebianco, A. (1988), *Political Parties: Organisation and Power* (Cambridge: Cambridge University Press).

Papadakis, E. (1983), 'The Green party in contemporary West German politics', *Political Quarterly*, 54.

Papadakis, E. (1984), *The Green Movement in West Germany* (London: Croom Helm).

Pappi, F-U. (1977), 'Sozialstruktur gesellschaftlicher Weltorientierung und Wahlabsicht', *Politische Vierteljahresschrift*, 18.

Pappi, F-U. (1993), 'Policy-Netze: Erscheinungsform moderner Politiksteuerung oder methodischer Ansatz?', *Politische Vierteljahresschrift*, Sonderheft, 24: 84-94.

Paterson, W. *et al.* (1989), *Developments in West German Politics* (Basingstoke: Macmillan).

Paterson, W. E. and Southern, D. (1991), *Governing Germany* (Oxford: Blackwell).

Paterson, W. E. (1996), 'Beyond semi-sovereignty: The new Germany in the new Europe', *German Politics*, 5, 2: 167–84.

Pickvance, C. and Pierre, J. (eds) (1990), *Challenges to Local Government* (Newbury Park: Sage).

Poguntke, T. (1989), 'An alternative politics?: The German Green Party in a comparative context', Doctoral Thesis, European University Institute, Florence.

Poguntke, T. (1993), *Alternative Politics: The German Green Party*, (Edinburgh: Edinburgh University Press).

Potthoff, H. (1991), 'Aufstieg und Niedergang der SPD', *Neue Gesellschaft/Frankfurter Hefte*, 38, 4.

Pridham, G. (ed.) (1986), *Coalition Behaviour in Theory and Practice* (Cambridge: Cambridge University Press).

Pridham, G. (1977), *Christian Democracy in Western Germany* (London: Croom Helm).

Rashke, J. (1993), *Krise der Grünen: Bilanz und Neubegin*. 2. verb. Aufl. Marburg: Schuren.

Rhodes, R. A. W. (1981), *Control and Power in Central-Local Government Relations* (Aldershot: Gower).

Rhodes, R. A. W. (1986a), *The National World of Local Government* (London: Allen & Unwin).

Rhodes, R. A. W. (1986b), 'Power Dependence, Policy Communities and Inter-governmental Networks', Essex Papers in Politics and Government, No. 30, University of Essex, Colchester.

Rhodes, R. A. W. and Marsh, D. (1992), 'Policy networks in British politics: A critique of existing approaches', in Marsh, D. and Rhodes, R. A. W. (eds), *Policy Networks in British Government* (Oxford: Clarendon Press).

Richardson J. J. and Jordan, A. G. (1979), *Governing under Pressure* (London: Robertson).

Riker, W. and Ordeshook, P.C. (1973), *An Introduction to Positive Political Theory* (Englewood Cliffs, NJ: Prentice-Hall).

Riker, W. H. (1980), 'Implications from the disequelibrium of majority rule for the study of institutions', *American Political Science Review*, 74: 432–46.

Riker, W. H. (1962), *The Theory of Political Coalitions* (New Haven: Yale University Press).

Roberts, G. (1989), 'Political parties and public policy', in Bulmer, S. (ed.), *The Changing Agenda of West German Public Policy* (London: Dartmouth).

Rose, R. (1991), *Bringing Freedom Back In: Rethinking Priorities of the Welfare State* (Glasgow: Centre for Public Policy, University of Strathclyde).

Ryan, A. (ed.) (1973), *The Philosophy of Social Explanation* (Oxford: Oxford University Press).

Sanders, D. and Herman, V. (1977), 'The stability and survival of Western governments', *Acta Politica*, 12: 346–77.

Sartori, G. (1994), *Comparative Constitutional Engineering: An Inquiry into Structures, Incentives and Outcomes* (New York: New York University Press).

Saunders, D. (1995), 'Behavioural Analysis', in Marsh, D. and Stoker, G. (eds), *Theory and Methods in Political Science* (Basingstoke: Macmillan).

Savage, L. J. (1954), *The Foundations of Statistics* (New York; London: John Wiley).

Scharf, T. (1994), *The German Greens: Challenging the Consensus* (Oxford: Berg).

Schmidt, M. (1992), 'Political consequences of unification', *West European Politics*, 15, 4: 1–15.

Schmitter, P. and Lehmbruch, G. (eds) (1979), *Trends towards Corporatist Intermediation* (Newbury Park: Sage).

Schneider, C. (1996), 'Abfallpolitische Richtungsentscheidungen mit Grenzwerten: Die technische Anleitung Siedlungsabfall im föderalen Prozess', Hannover: MA Thesis. Universität Hannover.

Schneider, V. (1988), 'Politiknetzwerke der Chemikalienkontrolle. Eine Analyse eiener transnationalen Politikentwicklung', European University Institute Series C. Berlin: de Gruyter.

Schorske, C. E. (1955), *German Social Democracy, 1905–1917* (Cambridge MA: Harvard University Press).

Sharpe, L. J. (1993), *The Rise of Meso Government in Europe* (Newbury Park: Sage).

Shepsle, K. (1979), 'Institutional arrangements and equilibrium in multidimensional voting models', *American Journal of Political Science*, 23: 27–60.

Silvia, S. J. (1993), '"Loosely coupled anarchy": The fragmentation of the Left', in Padgett, S. (ed.), *Parties and Party Systems in the New Germany* (Aldershot: Dartmouth).

Singer, O. (1991), 'The politics and economics of German Unification: from currency union to economic dichotomy', *German Politics*, 1, 1: 78–94.

Skou Andersen, M. (1994), *Governance by Green Taxes: Making Pollution Prevention Pay* (Manchester: Manchester University Press).

Smith, B. C. (1985), *Decentralisation: The Territorial Dimension of the State*, (London: Allen & Unwin).

Smith, G., Paterson, W. and Merkl, P. (eds) (1989), *Developments in West German Politics* (Basingstoke: Macmillan).

Smith, G. *et al.* (eds) (1992), *Developments in German Politics* (Basingstoke: Macmillan).

SPD Landesverband (1988), *Berlin ist Freiheit, Eine starke SPD für Berlin*, Wahlprogramme der Berliner SPD für die Wahlen zum Abgeordnetenhaus von Berlin am 29. Januar 1989, Beschlossen auf dem Landesparteitag am 15 October 1988.

SPD Landesverband (1989), *Berliner Koalitionsvereinbarung zwischen SPD und AL vom 13 March 1989.*

SPD Landesverband Niedersachsen (1990), *Koalitionsvereinbarung vom 19. Juni 1990, Der Landesverband Niedersachsen der Sozialdemokratischen Partei Deutschlands und der Landesverband die Grünen Niedersachsen.*

SPD Landesverband Niedersachsen (1990), *Sozial, ökologisch, stark. Landeswahlprogramm 1990.*

SPD (1998), *Arbeit. Innovation und Gerechtigkeit: SPD- Wahlprogramme für die Bundestagswahl 1998.*

SPD/Die Grünen (1998), *Aufbruch und Erneuerung. Deutschlands Weg ins 21, Jahrhundert.*

SPD (1999), *Der Weg nach vorne für Europas Sozialdemonkraten, Ein Vorschlag von Gerhard Schröder und Tony Blair.*

Der Spiegel magazine.

Statistisches Amt Niedersachsens (1990), *Statistischer Vierteljahresbericht Hannover, April–Juni 1990.* Heft II.

Statistisches Amt Niedersachsens (1994), *Statistischer Vierteljahresbericht Hannover, Janaur–März* Heft I.

Statistisches Bundesamt (various datasets).

Statistiches Landesamt Berlin (various datasets).

Statistiches Landesamt Niedersachsens (various datasets).

Strom, K. (1989), *Minority Government and Majority Rule* (Cambridge: Cambridge University Press).

Süddeutsche Zeitung newspaper.

Der Tageszeitung (TAZ) newspaper.

Tsebelis, G. (1990), *Nested Games: Rational Choice in Comparative Politics* (Berkeley, Los Angeles: University of California Press).

UmweltR. 9. A. 5533. *Umweltrecht* (Munich: Becke-Texte im dtv).

van Deth, J. W. and Geurts, P. A. T. M. (1989), 'Value orientation, left–right placement and voting', *European Journal of Political Research*, 6, 17: 17–34

Veen, H-J. (1993), 'The first all-German elections', in Padgett, S. (ed.), *Parties and Party Systems in the New Germany* (Aldershot: Dartmouth).

Verdener Aller-Zeitung newspaper.

von Beyme, K. (1984), *Political Parties in Western Democracies* (Aldershot: Gower).

von Beyme, K. (1985), 'Policy making in the Federal Republic of Germany: A systematic introduction', in von Beyme, K. and Schmidt, M. (eds), *Policy and Politics in the Federal Republic of Germany* (Aldershot: Gower).

von Beyme, K. (1991), *Das politische System der Bundesrepublic Deutschland nach der Vereinigung* (Munich: Piper).

von Neumann, J. and Morgenstern, O. (1947), *Theory of Games and Economic Behaviour* (Princeton, Guildford: Princeton University Press).

von Winter, T. (1990), 'Die Parteien und die Zukunft der Arbeit. Arbeitsgesellschaftliche Probleme in der Programmatik von SPD und CDU', *Leviathan*, Special Issue 11.

Ware, A. (ed.) (1987), *Political Parties: Electoral Change and Structural Response* (Oxford: Blackwell).

Warwick, P. (1988), 'Models of cabinet stability: A preliminary evaluation', paper presented at the annual meeting of the American Political Science Association, Washington DC.

Weale, A. (1992a), *The New Politics of Pollution* (Manchester: Manchester University Press).

Weale, A. (1992b), 'Vorsprung durch technik? The politics of German environmental regulation', in Dyson, K. (ed.), *The Politics of German Regulation* (Aldershot: Dartmouth).

Weale, A. (1999), 'European environmental policy by stealth: The dysfunctionality of functionalism?', *Environment and Planning C: Government Policy*, 17: 37–51.

Weidner, H. (1995), '25 Years of Modern Environmental Policy in Germany: Treading a Well-worn Path to the Top of the International Field', working paper, FS II 95–301, Wissenschaftszentrum Berlin für Sozialforschung, Berlin.

Wey, K-G. (1982), *Umweltpolitik in Deutschland: Kurze Geschichtedes Umweltschutzes in Deutschland seit 1900* (Opladen: Westdeutsche Verlag).

Wiesendahl, E. (1992), 'Volksparteien im Abstieg', *Aus Politik und Zeitgeschichte: Beilage zur Wochenzeitung Das Parlament*, 34–5/92: 3–14.

Index